More Praise for *Gardens*

T0278837

"God sees gardens in deserts, and through the witness of visionaries, gives us eyes to see them too and wills to join with others to cultivate them. Michael and Ken are imagineers, who both inspire and enlist us in the renovation mission."

—Steve Harper, retired seminary professor and author of *Coming Alive, Life in Christ*, and *Five Marks of a Methodist*, all from Abingdon Press

"In *Gardens in the Desert*, the authors present a compelling vision for how the church can flourish and not flounder in an increasingly complex and hostile world. Timely, insightful, and ultimately hopeful, *Gardens in the Desert* is a must-read for anyone who cares about the future of the church and its potential to bring healing to a parched planet. The authors' adaptive leadership framework charts a way forward that is both realistic and inspiring, reminding us that even in the most barren and inhospitable environments, vibrant gardens of faith and community can bloom and boom."

—Leonard Sweet, author, professor, preacher, publisher, proprietor of sanctuaryseaside.com, and founder of preachthestory.com

"While our world longs for connection and compassion, our congregations struggle to share God's grace. *Gardens in the Desert* expertly analyzes the changing climate to guide congregations on the urgent journey of adaptation. Beck and Carter draw from their vast knowledge, meaningful relationships, and compassionate wisdom in this unique resource."

—Laceye C. Warner, Royce and Jane Reynolds Professor of the Practice of Evangelism and Methodist Studies; Associate Dean for Wesleyan Engagement; Chair, Ministerial Division, Duke Divinity School, Durham, NC

"The church finds itself in a strange new land struggling to make sense of our faith in a culture that just doesn't care. Michael Beck and Ken Carter have set themselves the task of providing us with the tools we need to awaken the adaptive ecclesiology resident in all apostolic movements. The toolkit they've assembled is carefully and systematically laid out to help the church not only survive but thrive, to not only endure but flourish. Wise, inspiring, and practical."

—Michael Frost, founding director, Tinsley Institute, Morling College, Sydney, Australia

"We are never going back to the way things were. Michael Beck and Bishop Ken Carter provide wise guidance for church leaders seeking to adapt in these challenging times. I am recommending this book to all the church leaders that I work with."

—Mike Slaughter, Founder & Chief Strategist, Passionate Churches LLC

"As we grapple with the tremendous changes facing our Mainline Protestant Churches, Bishop Ken Carter and Rev. Dr. Michael Beck have thrown us a lifeline in their new book, *Gardens in the Desert: How the Adaptive Church Can Lead a Whole New Life*.

Gardens in the Desert is not just a theoretical exploration. It is a practical guide, as Carter and Beck skillfully blend secular Adaptive Leadership principles with cutting-edge research in church revitalization, providing a blueprint for any church seeking to reinvent itself.

Gardens in the Desert is a must-read for anyone serious about remaking their church. Pick it up now to begin the process of change and renewal!"

—Grant J Hagiya, President and Professor of Leadership and Innovation, Claremont School of Theology, Claremont, CA; United Methodist Bishop, retired

"It is an honor to endorse *Gardens in the Desert: How the Adaptive Church Can Lead a Whole New Life* by Michael Beck and Bishop Ken Carter. This inspiring and practical guide offers a fresh, scripture-rooted vision for church leaders navigating today's challenges. With wisdom drawn from Jeremiah 29, the authors provide actionable strategies for fostering adaptive leadership and cultivating meaningful relationships. Rich with practical ideas, illustrations, and frameworks, this book is an invaluable resource for anyone ready to embrace a vibrant, faith-filled future for their community."

—Lanette Plambeck, Bishop, Dakotas-Minnesota Area, UMC

Michael Adam Beck
Kenneth H. Carter Jr.

GARDENS IN THE DESERT

How the Adaptive Church
Can Lead a Whole New Life

Abingdon Press
Nashville

GARDENS IN THE DESERT:
HOW THE ADAPTIVE CHURCH CAN LEAD A WHOLE NEW LIFE

Copyright © 2024 by Abingdon Press

ISBN: 978-1-7910-3380-4

Library of Congress Control Number: 2024934278

Scripture quotations marked CEB are from the Common English Bible. Copyright © 2011 by the Common English Bible. All rights reserved. Used by permission. www.CommonEnglishBible.com.

Scripture quotations unless otherwise noted are taken from the New Revised Standard Version Updated Edition. Copyright © 2021 National Council of Churches of Christ in the United States of America. Used by permission. All rights reserved worldwide.

Scripture quotations marked (NIV) are taken from the Holy Bible, New International Version®, NIV®. Copyright © 1973, 1978, 1984, 2011 by Biblica, Inc.™ Used by permission of Zondervan. All rights reserved worldwide. www.zondervan.com The "NIV" and "New International Version" are trademarks registered in the United States Patent and Trademark Office by Biblica, Inc.™

Scripture quotations noted KJV are from The Authorized (King James) Version. Rights in the Authorized Version in the United Kingdom are vested in the Crown. Reproduced by permission of the Crown's patentee, Cambridge University Press.

MANUFACTURED IN THE UNITED STATES OF AMERICA

Dedication

Essential Friends in the Adaptive Journey

We would like to acknowledge friends who have encouraged us, inspired us, provoked us, and taught us in the work of adaptive ecclesiology.

Some of these friends are Piper Ramsey-Sumner, Audrey Warren, Michael Moynagh, Martyn Atkins, Luke Edwards, June Edwards, Sue Haupert-Johnson, Wayner Dickert, Gil Rendle, Alex Shanks, Cynthia Weems, Candace Lewis, Amy Coles, Kim Ingram, Cindy Thompson, Jeff and Jessica Taylor, David Allen, Alan Hirsch, Rich Robinson, Stephanie Moore Hand, Tiffany McCall, Heather Jallad, Susan Arnold, Jeff VanDyke, Rosario Picardo, Rob Hutchinson, Len Wilson, Robert G. Johnson, Graham Cray, Dave Male, Bener Agtarap, Chris and Jaidymar Smith, Grant Hagiya and Connie Shelton

Michael would like to thank Leonard Sweet, a mentor and friend who helped shape his ecclesiology, United Theological Seminary for allowing him to create a Fresh Expressions House of Studies that has served as a kind of laboratory for adaptive ecclesiology, and Path 1 at Discipleship Ministries for spreading these adaptations throughout the connection.

Ken would like to thank his students in the Introduction to Christian Leadership course in the Doctor of Ministry program at Duke Divinity School, and also David Goatley (now president of Fuller Theological Seminary), Will Willimon, Laceye Warner, and Edgardo Colon-Emeric of Duke Divinity School for the invitation to share this material with them. He would also like to thank the Emerging Community Pastor Cohort of the Western North Carolina Conference of The United Methodist Church, and Robb Webb and Kristen Richardson-Frick of the Duke Endowment for their strategic and material support of this work.

Lastly, and most importantly, we would like to thank our spouses, Jill Beck and Pam Carter, who are gifted ministers in their own rights, and who have lived this adaptation with us.

Contents

Cultivating Gardens of Wellbeing in the Desert of Exile

Build houses and live in them; plant gardens and eat what they produce. Take wives and have sons and daughters; take wives for your sons, and give your daughters in marriage, that they may bear sons and daughters; multiply there, and do not decrease. But seek the welfare of the city where I have sent you into exile, and pray to the Lord on its behalf, for in its welfare you will find your welfare.
—Jeremiah 29:5-7 (Emphasis added)

The world has changed all around us. Even before the global pandemic came along, we were facing the multiple and interconnected pandemics of systemic racism, inequality, poverty, climate change, political extremism, corrupt justice systems, an increase in mental illness, and the disintegration of church as we know it—just to name a few.

Shelly Rambo, a theologian who works in the discipline of trauma studies, suggests that in our contemporary setting, post-traumatic stress disorder (PTSD) is no longer only a diagnostic label for individuals in a suffering condition. Rather "it has become a way of naming the conditions of life more broadly."[1] Unresolved trauma spills out in patterns of harm and can be passed on generationally. We live in a traumatized age.

---

1. Stephanie N. Arel and Shelly Rambo (eds.), *Post-Traumatic Public Theology*, 1st ed. (Palgrave Macmillan, 2016), 9.

Gil Rendle, former senior vice president for the Texas Methodist Foundation as well as former senior consultant and director of consulting for the Alban Institute, refers to the season in which the church in the United States flourished as an "aberrant time." An aberration is not the norm; it is in fact "a departure from the normal state of affairs."[2] The conditions that caused the Christendom, attractional, propositional iteration of the church to thrive in the United States have changed.

It's as if the church we've known was formed in a jungle, but now we find ourselves in a desert. A jungle is a living system, with a multitude of life forms. A desert is also a living system with its own unique life forms and context. We now find ourselves in an entirely new ecosystem, and we must learn a new way of being for desert life. We will learn to get water from a cactus, and some of us will discover needles in our hands! We will learn to locate the oases of the Spirit. We will plant new kinds of gardens together. The church planted in jungle conditions is now learning how to live in a desert.

This is not a technical problem with a technical solution; this is an adaptive challenge. We find ourselves in a *wicked environment*. We mean wicked not in the sense of being evil or morally wrong but rather as a complex environment where "success" as we once conceived it is not the most likely outcome.

Consider the difference between "kind learning environments" and "wicked learning environments." In kind learning environments, patterns repeat consistently, and feedback is accurate and rapidly obtainable. In "wicked learning environments" there may not be repetitive patterns; the rules of the game are unclear; the status quo changes; and feedback is often delayed, inaccurate, or both.[3]

Wicked learning environments thrust us into an adaptive challenge. While some of our knowledge and skills will transfer, many will not. We

---

2. Gil Rendle, *Quietly Courageous: Leading the Church in a Changing World* (Lanham, MD: Rowman & Littlefield, 2019), 21–23.

3. Robin Hogarth, et al., "The Two Settings of Kind and Wicked Learning Environments," *Current Directions in Psychological Science* 24, no. 5 (2015): 379–85, 379.

all operate from what Peter Senge, an MIT systems scientist, calls a particular "mental model," which contains deeply held internal images of how the world works, images that can limit us to familiar ways of thinking and acting.[4] But now we are called to *metanoia*, a transformative change of heart and mind. We need to see the emerging context with the soft eyes of a learner.

We also benefit from different expressions of leadership for this scenario.

For instance, *relational leadership* holds everyone together under the stress of the new challenges. *Implemental leadership* knows how to fix the technical problems that arise. *Interpretive leadership* gives us the ability to locate ourselves in God's unfolding story and name our reality, for example, asking, "Hey did anyone notice things have changed?"

There's no question that we need *relational, implemental,* and *interpretive* leadership. But the most important kind of leadership needed in a wicked domain is *adaptive leadership.*

Adaptive leadership helps us operate in the uncertainties, improvise, and find a way forward. It frees us to engage the context in new ways, ask natives for directions, and collaborate with new coalitions . . . hitchhiking together toward a future destination! This requires communities of *shared leadership*, in which power is "distributed" evenly among teams. Thus, influence and decision-making are not consolidated in a single individual in a managerial role only but rather in an interactive dynamic in which any particular person will fluctuate between being a leader and a follower.

Adaptive leadership, then, concerns an innate ability to adapt to diverse, chaotic, and complex environments, thereby assisting organizations and individuals in dealing with consequential changes in uncertain times, when no clear answers are forthcoming.[5]

---

4.   Peter M. Senge, *The Fifth Discipline: The Art and Practice of the Learning Organization* (New York: Doubleday/Currency, 2006), 163.

5.   Mark Lau Branson, "Interpretive Leadership During Social Dislocation: Jeremiah and Social Imaginary," *Journal of Religious Leadership* 8, no. 1 (2009): 27–48, 29.

Jürgen Habermas, German social theorist and philosopher, discusses the concept of "lifeworlds."[6] Lifeworlds include the conceptual backgrounds, assumptions, linguistic fields, and social imaginaries that people inhabit as a living space, each of which contains assumed structures of meaning that are largely unconscious, yet serve as the basis of any efforts at communication and cooperative activities.[7] These lifeworlds are the ways people imagine their social existence, how they relate to others, how things go on between them and others; they also encompass their normal expectations and the underlying notions of these expectations. These lifeworlds shape our mental models.

Jeremiah and the people of Israel found themselves in a new lifeworld. They were taken into captivity, exiled from the promised land. While many prophets are soothsaying, assuring the people it will all be over soon, Jeremiah's message is different. He instructs the people to dig in, start families, plant gardens, and prepare for the long haul. He instructs the people to embrace the new lifeworld where they find themselves and "seek the welfare of the city where I have sent you into exile, and pray to the Lord on its behalf, for in its welfare you will find your welfare" (Jer 29:5-7).

Jeremiah encourages a people in exile to seek their new neighbors' wellbeing and flourishing.

We could break down the heart of Jeremiah's instructions and how they might inform our situation today in the following way:

1. **Adopt a posture of permanence: build houses and live in them.** In Jeremiah's context, this was about not trying to run off to Egypt or anticipate returning to Israel anytime soon. It was a call to embrace the new lifeworld of exile. For us, this is about learning new ways to do life with the people, neighborhoods, and networks where we dwell. Our reality has changed, and we must learn how to adapt.

---

6. Jürgen Habermas, *The Theory of Communicative Action* (Boston, MA: Beacon, 1984).

7. Branson, "Interpretive Leadership During Social Dislocation," 29.

2. Plant green spaces and eat. For Jeremiah, this was about set-tling in, utilizing the land, and embracing the new ecosystem as home. But also, it was about experimenting with planting new kinds of gardens and in new soils. For us, cultivating green spaces is about finding ways to form incarnational community with the natives. It takes on a short-term, experimental ap-proach to life. Let's plant new things, share our recipes, and eat the food made by our own cooking.

3. Establish families among the people. Essentially, many peo-ple in Babylonian captivity would never return to their home-land. Jeremiah encourages them to start families and multiply in the reality of exile. This would require more than surface-level interaction with their captors. Instead, they would need to work, form partnerships, and flourish in these conditions. Churches can slip into a mindset of presentism and exclusiv-ism. We stop thinking generationally. We neglect the calling to pass our faith to our children. It becomes all about our prefer-ences. We can also function as a closed system, neglecting to interact with the larger community. This is a call to enter the world of the "other" as humble learners and embrace a posture of vulnerability and interdependence. It's a commitment to think generatively.

4. Seek the wellbeing of the other = the city where you are. This is breaking away from the *Lex talionis*—the law of "measure for measure"; an eye-for-an-eye, tooth-for-a-tooth kind of theol-ogy from the Levitical covenant (Exod 21:24). This is moving toward a "love your enemy and bless those who persecute you" kind of posture. It's hard to imagine the experience of watch-ing foreign invaders destroy our sacred spaces and parade us as captives taken out of our homeland as trophies of war, but this is exactly what happened to Israel. James Cone, widely con-sidered the father of black liberation theology, demonstrates that the black diasporic experience through four hundred ter-rible years of the transatlantic slave trade is a kind of captiv-ity and exile that persists to this day.[8] For an exile of biblical

---

8. James H. Cone, *The Spirituals and the Blues: An Interpretation* (Maryknoll, NY: Orbis, 1999).

proportions, inhabitants in the United States need to look no further than their own blood-soaked backyards.

So, today, to use the term exile to describe the state of most Christians lacks sociohistorical sensitivity. Christians in the West are not in that kind of a hostile takeover, and yet the church has certainly found itself in a kind of exile of irrelevance and decline. Thus, George Lings suggests that the analogy of exile is helpful for the Western church, in the sense that we have moved from a culture where being a Christian was either expected or tolerated, to a culture that is now largely indifferent or hostile.[9] Some of this results from the church's self-inflicted wounds and the harm we have done to one another. Thus, we find ourselves in a new space. We must go beyond our attractional Christendom mentality of imagining that "they will come to us." We must genuinely find ways to inhabit our communities and seek the wellbeing of the entire ecosystem, not just the church we inhabit. We must ask the questions: Who is my other? and How can I be with them? As Margaret Wheatley suggests, to seek the wellbeing of the people is to be little "islands of sanity" and healing in a sea of trauma.[10]

5. **Disregard the dominant wishful thinking. It is deception.** Jeremiah's greatest opponents came from within his own religious and political system. He had to oppose the priests of his day and the institutional big-guns who were giving a sugar-coated prosperity narrative about the way things were: "Listen, Hananiah! The Lord has not sent you, yet you have persuaded this nation to trust in lies" (Jer 28:13-15). The religious leaders were essentially saying, "Everything will be just fine; we will be going home real soon!" Jeremiah's bold counter-narrative was, "No! We aren't going home, not for a long time anyway."

As he listens to God's voice, Jeremiah's courage leads him to an alternative interpretation. Modern-day prophets in the school

---

9. George Lings, "A Golden Opportunity: Revisiting the Story So Far," *Encounters on the Edge* 50 (2011).

10. Margaret J. Wheatley, *Who Do We Choose to Be? Facing Reality, Claiming Leadership, Restoring Sanity* (Oakland, CA: Berrett-Koehler, 2017).

of Jeremiah help us to name our affinity for nostalgia; if we keep doing what we have always done, surely the people will return to pack our pews once again. This is a profound example of work avoidance.

The people in exile found themselves in an adaptive challenge, and they learned to become an *adaptive community*.

Again, while many of us are clearly unable to imagine the horrors of subjugation and exile, perhaps we can still learn from this scenario. The reality of post-Christendom has been well documented. Theologians, philosophers, and sociologists concur that societies have now entered a post-Christian or post-establishment Christian reality in the Western world. Yet, Willie James Jennings pushes against the common assumptions of what this often means for Eurotribal peoples. He contends that, clearly, the easy alignment of Protestantism with the quasi-religious sensibilities of the nation-state has vanished. But he also writes:

> Whatever the claimed cause of this situation for the church in the modern "post-Christendom" world, the conclusion is the same: Western Christians are a minority, an exilic people in a strange land. While the old Anglo-Saxon Protestant hegemony may be over, such readings of the reality of Christian existence in the West are painfully superficial. They bypass the deeper realities of Western Christian sensibilities, identities, and habits of mind which continue to channel patterns of colonialist dominance.[11]

A true adaptive ecclesiology cannot accept this superficial reading of post-Christendom. It must confront and discard the harmful elements in the very DNA of Christendom itself. It must come to terms with racism, patriarchy, ableism, and homophobia. The church must see its legacy of oppression and colonialism.

Serene Jones, in mapping feminist theory and theology, reminds us that oppression is not always easy to name. She says: "In fact, because oppression affects the very way one thinks about oneself and one's world, it is

---

11. Willie J. Jennings, *The Christian Imagination: Theology and the Origins of Race* (New Haven, CT: Yale University Press, 2010), 8.

often quite difficult to even see, much less name. Oppression makes itself invisible, distorts vision, and twists thought. Similarly, it is hard to envision new ways of living when everything one experiences is rooted in old, oppressive forms of knowing and acting."[12] Adaptive ecclesiology requires us to see and name oppression and seek new forms of knowing and acting. This ultimately requires new forms of church as well.

To simplify: the challenge of re-evangelizing a previously so-called Christian context is a different challenge than evangelizing a new context. It's not a journey to the promised land, it's the experience of being exiled from the promised land we once inhabited. It's a change of lifeworlds from what we knew before.

Every local congregation inhabits its own kind of lifeworld, of which it is largely unaware. Even the language we use, largely a product of our lifeworld, occurs at a subconscious level with layers of assumed meaning.

The big idea of this book is that congregations, networks, and denominations themselves must adapt to the new ecosystem. We need to awaken the *adaptive ecclesiology* embedded in the scriptures and expressed in diverse ways across church history.

Adaptive refers to a trait that improves an organism's fitness for survival and flourishing.

Ecclesiology refers simply to the study of the church, but this can also focus on the origins of Christianity, its relationship to Jesus, its role in salvation, its polity, its discipline, its eschatology, its nature, and its leadership.

In describing adaptive leadership as the "practice of mobilizing people to tackle tough challenges and thrive," Ronald Heifetz, Alexander Grashow, and Marty Linsky draw from evolutionary biology. They propose that successful adaptation has three characteristics:

1. it preserves the DNA essential for the species' continued survival;

---

12. Serene Jones, *Feminist Theory and Christian Theology: Cartographies of Grace. Guides to Theological Inquiry* (Minneapolis, MN: Fortress, 2000), 3.

2. it discards (reregulates or rearranges) the DNA that no longer serves the species' current needs;

3. it creates DNA arrangements that give the species' the ability to flourish in new ways and in more challenging environments.[13]

Heifetz and Linsky are the authors of two revolutionary books, *Leadership Without Easy Answers* and *Leadership on the Line*. They introduced the adaptive leadership model at Harvard University. As business leaders, they generated the model from the realization that the single-figure, top-down leadership model is ineffective and impractical. Adaptive leadership became an emerging model that embraced disruption, change, experimentation, and innovation. In their work, they sought to help companies handle challenges and adapt to evolving environments. We have been profoundly impacted in our own leadership by their work.

We also want to be cautious about merely adopting ideas from the corporate world and applying them haphazardly to the church. So, here, we want to ground key ideas from adaptive leadership theory in scripture, tradition, reason, and experience. Finally, we want to suggest practical ways we can apply these inspired ideas to our massively changed landscape in a pandemic age. We do this as active practitioners who spend time both on the ground in local ministry contexts, and as denominational leaders in the balcony. One focus of our work together is in the area of Fresh Expressions of Church, which we see as a form and movement of adaptive ecclesiology.

In 2004, Bishop Graham Cray and his team produced the Mission-Shaped Church report. They recognized the level of change, and that new forms of church, which they first called "fresh expressions," would need to exist alongside inherited models of church in a "mixed economy."[14]

13.   Ronald A. Heifetz, et al., *The Practice of Adaptive Leadership: Tools and Tactics for Changing Your Organization and the World* (Boston, MA: Harvard Business, 2009), 14.

14.   Graham Cray, *Mission-Shaped Church: Church Planting and Fresh Expressions in a Changing Context* (New York: Seabury, 2010), 100.

The authors were responding to a shift away from the parish-based assumptions about church (i.e., because people live here, they will become members) to a deeper awareness of changing patterns of behavior and the power of emergent networks. The report has now become an international bestseller and is credited with transforming the ecclesiology of the Church of England. The fruit of Mission-Shaped Church is seen in the development of thousands of fresh expressions, and in how it catalyzed similar initiatives in Australia, Canada, mainland Europe, South Africa, the United States, and elsewhere.[15]

A mixed economy refers to a diversity of ecclesial forms in which fresh expressions of church exist alongside inherited forms in relationships of mutual respect and support. This term has largely fallen out of favor and been replaced by mixed ecology, which has the same meaning but is more agrarian and organic in nature. We believe there is a further movement, which we call a "blended ecology of church," in which fresh expressions of church live in symbiotic relationship with inherited forms of church in such a way that combining these modes over time blend to create a nascent form. This terminology speaks more potently to the new prevalence of blended family units, more fluid conceptions of identity, the creative process, current cultural realities, and the ancient agrarian language of Jesus. This is a helpful way to understand an adaptive ecclesiology.

We want to note that a similar movement that parallels Fresh Expressions also predates the latter by decades. It flows from the work of the liberation theologians of Latin America like Leonard Boff. Boff is a Franciscan priest who describes the "base ecclesial communities" of Brazil in his book *Ecclesiogenesis: The Base Communities Reinvent the Church*. He employs the language of the basic community (as described in the seminar held in Maringá, Brazil, from May 1 to 3, 1972, which examined these communities) as "a group, or complex of groups, of people in which a primary, personal relationship of brotherly and sisterly communion obtains,

---

15. Michael Moynagh, *Church in Life: Emergence, Ecclesiology and Entrepreneurship* (London: SCM, 2017), 2.

and which lives the totality of the life of the church, as expressed in service, celebration, and evangelization."[16]

There is deep resonance among these movements, and we will seek to integrate learnings into an adaptive ecclesiology.

In serving The United Methodist Church, one of us as bishop and the other as director of the fresh expressions movement, we have sought to embrace this adaptive way of being church. We believe it remains central to a vision for a thriving church in the future.

In this book we will integrate our learnings from the past decade and offer a way forward as we seek to follow our adaptive God—a God of incarnation, mission, and resurrection—so that we might become an adaptive church. We seek to become a church that is flourishing in a changed mission reality, one that is humble, generative, willing to experiment, and passionate about the well-being of the people and the places where we live. We aim to be a church that springs up like gardens in the desert. We believe that local congregations can become outward and visible signs of healing and new creation in a landscape marked by trauma and disorientation.

And we believe God has planted us now in each of our contexts to hear again the voice of the prophet and in the process to discover that we are also the ones who are being healed.

---

16.   Leonardo Boff, *Ecclesiogenesis: The Base Communities Reinvent the Church* (Maryknoll, NY: Orbis, 1986), 25.

CHAPTER ONE

Preserve

For where two or three are gathered in my name, I am there among them.
—Matthew 18:20

Adaptive Ecclesiology Expands Our Capacity to Thrive as a Church

"Adaptive leadership is the practice of mobilizing people to tackle tough challenges and thrive."[1]

To thrive, according to Heifetz, Grashow, and Linsky, we must take three actions:

1. preserve the essential DNA,

2. discard the DNA that no longer serves our needs, and

3. create DNA arrangements that enable us to flourish in new ways and in new environments.

What We Keep

What does this mean for an adaptive ecclesiology? What do we most want to preserve in our DNA? We are blessed with a deep, rich, and life-long understanding of the grace of God. We are strengthened by a sense

---

1.   Ronald A. Heifetz, et al., *The Practice of Adaptive Leadership: Tools and Tactics for Changing Your Organization and the World* (Boston, MA: Harvard Business, 2009), 14.

of connection and conferencing with other disciples. We grow through a humble but concerted desire to journey toward holiness. This leads to an external focus on the world beyond us, and on the people who are not present among us. And these realities are sustained by an ordering of ministry for the sake of the mission.

"In biological adaptations," Heifetz, Grashow, and Linsky note, "though DNA changes may radically expand the species' capacity to thrive, the actual amount of DNA that changes is miniscule."

And, so, an adaptive ecclesiology preserves much of the tradition, even as it creates essential changes.

What We Lay Aside

What do we to need to discard, to lay aside, in an adaptive church? We can lay aside a thick, monolithic book of polity. We can discard the privilege that we give to our own cultural contexts at the expense of others. We can learn to see law through the lens of grace. We can purge the "isms" that do systemic harm to whole groups of people. We can let go of the desire to be a heroic solo leader. We can dismantle the idols of the successful, market-driven church.

These realities have come to define us more than we would care to admit, and yet they contribute very little, if at all, to the faithful and fruitful living and sharing of the gospel.

So, what do you need to lay aside, to use the language of Hebrews 12:1-2? What is weighing on us, as leaders, as communities? What can we live more freely and joyfully without?

What We Rearrange

How do we create new DNA arrangements that enable us to flourish in new ways and in new environments?

If we open our eyes, can we see the "new thing" God promises in Isaiah 43? There are fresh expressions of church, which could be understood as the ancestors of class meetings and field preaching. There are gatherings of God's people in "third-places," which have echoes of a people who migrated from temples to synagogues. There are blended ecologies, traditions, and innovations—modern and postmodern, ancient and future. There are contemplatives and activists, the inward journey shaping the outward journey, and vice versa.

The adaptive church moves into new environments, beyond its walls. The church shapes the community, and in the same way it is shaped by the world beyond it. The adaptive church experiences the prevenient grace of God that is present in the world beyond the church's walls.

And, along the way, our DNA gets rearranged. This is adaptive ecclesiology. We cling to much of a tradition that we love. We let go of the parts of our tradition that no longer serve us or the mission. We are transformed as we engage in the mission.

The "Why" of an Adaptive Ecclesiology

Ronald Heifetz speaks of adaptation as actually requiring very little change in the evolutionary process. To meaningfully design a new ecclesial ecosystem (church) will require that it have enough commonality with the past to be recognizable. At the same time, progression is essential, lest we remain stuck in environments that are no longer tenable or worthy of perpetuation (this would be nostalgia).

The competing commitments are both how we are shaped by culture (Rabbi Jonathan Sacks speaks of the cultural climate change from "we" to "I") and how we justify a continuity of privilege and retention of power.

Creation requires living in a healthy tension between movements and institutions; individual practices; the need for connection with others; and relationships between convictions and beliefs, actions and practices (what Wesley would have called "Practical Divinity").

The need to redesign our practices asks us to see both what is a particular tradition's gift to the larger body of Christ and what is that same tradition's gift to the world beyond the church. These are, in some instances,

3

like the treasures (personal and social holiness, connection, etc.) hidden in our own backyards that we have taken for granted. Yet they need continual interpretation. For example, the Wesleyan gift to the body of Christ was spreading scriptural holiness and reforming the nation. Scriptural holiness requires definition and redefinition; reforming the nation is historical and contextual.

Each generation must reinterpret the embodiment of the following general rules.

- Do no harm: What does it mean for Methodists in the twenty-first century to "do no harm" in a landscape in which most view the church as guilty of doing great harm?

- Do good: In a scenario in which there is no significant correlation between church attendance and increased compassion, what does doing good look like?

- Attend to all the ordinances of God: Can we reimagine the what, when, and where of worship? Can "searching the scriptures" look like dialogue and reflection on the Jesus story? Can personal prayer be facilitated and deepened through an app? Can family prayer take into account the familial shifts into blended and single-parent families, or queer couples? What does regular fasting look like in an attention economy? Can the sacraments be duly administered in a tattoo parlor, a burrito shop, a dog park, or a rehab center's chemical dependency unit?

The practices of an adaptive ecclesiology shape how a church remains relevant (in the best sense of that word), incarnational, and vital. Practices are the ways in which the church is a movement; the institutional forms are more about boundaries, governance, and sustenance. One sees an adaptive ecclesiology within the development of the New Testament itself—an organic body with diverse gifts (1 Corinthians) over time gives way to pastoral letters (1 and 2 Timothy) where there are developed leadership roles and offices of ministry. We assume that the adaptive ecclesiology in the New Testament is a response to the gifts of God's people and the needs of the mission.

There are factors that get in the way of adaptation or innovation. Our resistance to context prevents the church's flourishing in some kinds of soils. Our hesitation in risk-taking leads to missed opportunities. Our privatization of religion leads to a therapeutic deism and our consequent divorce from the public spaces where our voices are needed.

You might take a moment and list the mindsets, habits, and structures that prevent adaptation.

At the same time, it is essential that we dwell for a time in the gifts of our good and generous Triune God: our creation in God's image; our liberation from bondage; our proximity to the voices of prophets who call us to repentance; our access to the means of grace; our participation in connection and *koinonia*; our relationship to Jesus Christ, our Savior, and the pouring out of the Holy Spirit.

These gifts are the constants, the unchanging DNA that is our identity, our birthright. And alongside these gifts is a calling not to bury them in the ground or hide them under a basket. The adaptation allows for the possibility that those outside of our churches will see, hear, believe, and follow.

These gifts form the foundation of an adaptive church.

Cleaning Out the Time Capsule

Imagine if someone were to take some cassette tapes, pagers, fanny packs, parachute pants, a Sega Genesis, Walkman, and a Bible; then, write a note that said, "Hello from 2024!" and place them all in a time capsule, and bury it. One day, someone in a future generation would recover that time capsule. They might behold those artifacts with awe and say, "So this is what 2024 was all about!"

Obviously, those items would not be accurate reflections of 2024, more like accurate reflections of the 1980s and 1990s (no 1990s renaissance based on those artifacts please!). Yet, in a sense, local churches can become that time capsule. Some of what we are preserving as the "church" is not an accurate reflection of the church at all, but a finite, culturally specific brand of the church, from one perspective in time and place. There is a deeper narrative that has been somewhat buried.

Part of discerning the essential DNA and rediscovering our *why* is about cleaning out the clutter that has been collected in a local church over time. Through the process of listening and exchanging questions, we can begin to sense the health of the inherited congregation. We also will begin to see the parts of the past that are obstructing the congregation's future. Now comes the tough work of throwing out the parachute pants, beepers, Walkmans, fanny packs, and Ataris cluttering the church's time capsule. This decluttering process allows the congregation to have a conversation to strip down to the church's essential DNA. This is where the work gets hard, but it can also have a powerful awakening effect on the congregation.

This allows a church to begin exploring what Alan Roxburgh describes as recovering the legitimating narrative, or Tod Bolsinger's references to the recommitment of core ideology.[2] Inevitably, we are going to discover some stuff in the time capsule that, while it may have been incredibly valuable for a specific time or context, no longer serves a purpose. Some of the things local churches hold onto are like wanting to keep using pagers even though pocket-sized super-computers called iPhones are available. People are unfortunately all too willing to die on those hills. This will require interpretive leadership that can lead a congregation to look deeper and establish the church's meaning and purpose.

What Is Church?

To refer again to the four words of the Nicene Creed (whose 1700th anniversary year is 2025) that capture the essential ingredients of the church: one, holy, catholic, and apostolic. Those four words are prominent themes throughout the whole scriptural witness. The church is a

---

2. Tod E. Bolsinger, *Canoeing the Mountains: Christian Leadership in Uncharted Territory* (Downers Grove, IL: IVP, 2016), 94.

connected (catholic) and *unified* (one) community of people; it is a community that reflects the very heart, character, and behavior of a *holy* God; and it is a community *sent* (apostolic) in mission to the world. Any church vision statement, mission, or purpose that doesn't include these ingredients is missing something absolutely essential.

A community that is one and catholic, whose behavior is shaped by an interaction with a holy God and is sent out to be this community in and among the world—that's what the creators of the Nicene Creed thought was essential DNA. Many churches can fall into a kind of amnesia over each of these marks; however, the one most glaringly absent in most congregations is sentness.

In the Fresh Expressions movement, we often lead an exercise called "What is Church?," where we give participants a list that includes some of the following words:

Sanctuary	Sunday School	Youth Ministry
Jesus	Coffee	God
Worship service	Holy Spirit	VBS
Children's Ministry	Choir	Bible
Music	Potluck dinners	Baptism
Prayer	Preacher	Mission
Women's Ministry	Communion	Hospitality
Bible Study	Evangelism	Fellowship
Softball team	Outreach	Committees
Organ	Money	Worship Band
Book of Common Worship	Book of Discipline	Offering
Hymnal	Nursery	Mission trips

We then ask them to eliminate all non-essential elements. For instance, if you were being parachute-dropped into a new context to plant a church, what essentials would constitute a true church of Jesus Christ?

7

Incredibly, preachers, bands, books of discipline or worship, and committees are often the first to go, although coffee and potlucks seem to be universal must-haves across denominations and races—rightfully so! What would the first apostles have accomplished without coffee and potlucks?

Almost without fail, most groups strip the church down to Jesus, God, and the Holy Spirit; many keep the Bible and the sacraments . . . and that's about it. When you think about it, how much of what we consider to be the church really has any basis in scripture and the practices of the early church?

This exercise is about getting down to the core DNA. For the church to adapt to the changing landscape, we need to decide what are the essentials we want to place in the time capsule to pass down to future generations. In many cases, we are planting the seeds of the church to come. This is the gift of movements like Fresh Expressions of Church. As we listen, love, and cultivate these grace-centered communities of inclusion and lay empowerment, we see a new ecosystem of church beginning to take root. The seeds of these communities contain core Wesleyan DNA, but their incarnational nature takes on the aspects and rhythms of the context. The same could be said of the Base Ecclesial Communities of Latin America. To adapt to the new missional context, we will need to reimagine the church in this way.

The Book of Discipline of The United Methodist Church defines the local church as a "community of true believers under the Lordship of Christ."[3] We believe this is a definition that gets down to the core DNA.

The greatest description of a minimal ecclesiology was provided by Jesus himself: "For where two or three are gathered in my name, I am there among them" (Matt 18:20). Where people are gathering around the risen Jesus as a community of love and forgiveness, there is the church.

---

3. *The Book of Discipline of The United Methodist Church 2016* (Nashville, TN: The United Methodist Publishing House, 2016), 147.

CHAPTER TWO

Discard

Therefore, keep awake—for you do not know when the master of the house will come,
in the evening, or at midnight, or at cockcrow, or at dawn, or else he may find you
asleep when he comes suddenly. And what I say to you I say to all: Keep awake.
—Mark 13:35-37

When we go about mission in the *name* of Jesus, but not in the *way* of Jesus, we do harm. Sometimes the non-essential DNA is not only unhelpful; it can be harmful.

Mission across Christian history has some blemishes to deal with. Consider, for instance, the "replacement model," a missionary method that attempted to "wipe the slate clean." Missionaries, with imperial support, were sent to replace the local or indigenous culture with "Christian" culture. An example often cited is the conquest of the so-called "New World" (Latin America 1493–1800), in which native religions were seen as animalistic, demonic, and idolatrous. Christian Spaniards viewed themselves as commissioned by God to propagate the faith, as "divine providence." This led to widespread abuse, bloodshed, and enslavement.[1]

Or consider the "ennoblement model" of mission in which the missionary's culture was viewed as superior and the goal was "elevating the recipient culture" to a shared place of ennoblement. An example is the General Evangelical Protestant Mission Association that began in 1884. The missionary worked with the country's intelligentsia to increase literary,

---

1. Henning Wrogemann, *Intercultural Theology: Intercultural Hermeneutics* (Downers Grove, IL: IVP, 2016), 259–320.

educational, and spiritual growth, opening kindergartens, hospitals, and nursing homes.

The progressive development of the world was facilitated through Christianity . . . God's kingdom on earth. "Culture" had elitist undertones, with Europeans and North Americans being considered superior. Missionaries were academically educated, and cultures would be advanced through means of education until they reached the "pinnacle" of Euro-Christian culture.[2] In the nationalist narrative of mission and evangelism, churches become the handmaiden of empire. We have seen this more recently with the rise of Christian nationalism in the United States.

The flaws and heartbreak of these examples are obvious.

The missional church conversation in recent decades was an attempt to divorce mission from a colonial, attractional, propositional form of Christendom concerned with expansion, hierarchical power, and "conversion of the heathen." Yet even this well-intentioned movement has been hijacked and used by people at theological extremes to advance their agenda and cause further harm.

Consider the phrase "The Gospel and Our Culture," To which "culture" are they referring? And who constitutes the "our"? It is a culture marked by whiteness with little input from liberation theologians. While earlier gatherings of mission councils emphasized listening to Latin American and other so-called "third-world" theologians, this shifted at the Lausanne Congress on World Evangelization (1974). The Lausanne Covenant doubled down on a vision of being evangelical that had strong conservative tendencies and minimized contextuality, dialogue, and saw social action as secondary to the core task of evangelizing the entire world. It also adopted a statement on scripture as inerrant and infallible.[3]

As we suggested earlier, one aspect of the harmful DNA in Western Christianity involves racism. As Isabel Wilkerson explains, "Just as DNA is the code of instructions for cell development, caste is the operating

---

2. Wrogemann, *Intercultural Theology,* 259–320.

3. Henning Wrogemann, *Intercultural Theology—Theologies of Mission,* vol. 2 (Downers Grove, IL: IVP, 2018), 115–25.

system for economic, political, and social interaction in the United States from the time of its gestation."[4] Wilkerson demonstrates that the US social structure is a racial caste system. Our colleague Dr. Stephanie Moore-Hand calls this a kind of invisible pyramid of racialization, and she points to how churches have been complicit in creating and sustaining it.[5]

W. E. B. Du Bois describes the paradox well: "From the day of its birth, the anomaly of slavery plagued a nation which asserted the equality of all men, and sought to derive powers of government from the consent of the governed. Within the sound of the voices of those who said this lived more than half a million black slaves, forming nearly one-fifth of the population of a new nation."[6]

In *Jesus and John Wayne*, Kristen Du Mez analyzes how evangelicals in the United States formed a position that it was not the role of government to interfere in issues of racial justice. They tended to emphasize that "only Jesus could change human hearts." Thus, when it came to issues like racism, "Many evangelicals, too, found it hard to accept that the sin of racism ran deep through the nation's history. To concede this seemed unpatriotic. Having embraced the idea of America as a 'Christian nation,' it was hard to accept a critique of the nation as fundamental as that advanced by the civil rights movement."[7]

Unfortunately, the attempted minimization of the voices of liberation theologians has limited the missional church conversation. Liberation theologians often emphasize social justice and a holistic vision of salvation as core aspects of mission and evangelization. As Elaine Heath writes, "Evangelism is not good news until it is good news for all of creation, for humanity, animals, plants, water, and soil, for the earth that God created

---

4. Isabel Wilkerson, *The Origins of Our Discontents* (New York: Random House, 2020), 25.

5. Michael Adam Beck and Stephanie Moore Hand, *Doing Justice Together* (Nashville: Abingdon, 2024).

6. W. E. B. Du Bois, *Black Reconstruction in America: Toward a History of the Part Which Black Folk Played in the Attempt to Reconstruct Democracy in America, 1860—1880* (London: Oxford University Press, 2014), 23.

7. Kristin Kobes Du Mez, *Jesus and John Wayne* (New York: Liveright, 2020), 27.

and called good."[8] The missional church has been utilized by the church growth movement, employing a skewed version of the "homogenous unit principle" that encourages segregationist tendencies. Critics claim it is guilty of tokenism, virtue signaling, and monetization in the neoliberal capital stream.[9]

Dr Keri Day, Professor of Constructive Theology and African American Religion, demonstrates how neoliberal capitalism is the overarching structure that preserves global inequity. She writes: "Our religious and moral imaginations are imprisoned to the fundamental market rationality of atomic individualism, which makes questions of caring relations seem idealistic and even naïve. We are often unable to imagine deeper modes of social connectedness or cooperation, as the grid of social intelligence that neoliberalism offers us is based on the pessimistic premise of radical individual self-interest."[10]

For some, the Western church has failed to offer an alternative vision of communal life apart from atomic individualism. It is limited by an imagination that fails to enable new and deeper modes of connectedness and cooperation. It aligns with existing political systems without prophetically interrogating those systems.

As Gustavo Gutiérrez notes, clergy in the Global South see challenging unjust political and economic systems as integral to their calling. One aspect of liberation theology from its genesis is a new dimension that places many priests "in a relationship of subversion regarding the existing social order."[11] As Leonard Boff demonstrates with the Base Ecclesial Communities, these expressions have an orientation toward justice. Boff writes: "But to be a good Christian, it is necessary to be concerned with social justice, and social justice is a political reality. In order to achieve this

---

8. Elaine Heath, *Mystic Way of Evangelism* (Grand Rapids, MI: Baker, 2008), 73.

9. Wrogemann, *Intercultural Theology—Theologies of Mission*, vol. 2, 115–25.

10. Keri Day, *Religious Resistance to Neoliberalism: Womanist and Black Feminist Perspectives* (London: Palgrave Macmillan, 2015), 12.

11. Gustavo Gutiérrez, *A Theology of Liberation: History, Politics, and Salvation* (Maryknoll, NY: Orbis, 1988), 118.

social justice, so wanting in today's discriminatory society, one must live the faith as a factor of transformation of social relationships."[12]

Keri Day reminds us that "love is not merely an ideal sentiment but a concrete revolutionary practice."[13] And Howard Thurman wisely states that, "The first step toward love is a common sharing of a sense of mutual worth and value. This cannot be discovered in a vacuum or in a series of artificial or hypothetical relationships. It has to be in a real situation, natural, free."[14]

Heath is worth quoting at length here:

> There is no greater challenge to the church in the night than to relinquish its idolatrous and syncretistic attachment to sexism, racism, and classism, for this trio of evil ideologies has been embedded in the American church from the time Christianity made its way across the Atlantic with the first explorers. The history of the church in America is, along with other stories, a long story of church-sanctioned injustice as women and ethnic minorities have been forced to live their faith from the margins. It is a story of Christians owning, raping, and whipping slaves, of using black women as breeders to expand the slave industry. It is a story of the genocide of countless Native Americans in the name of Manifest Destiny. It is a story of denominations forming explicitly to serve one race while excluding others, and of congregations moving from their 'changing' neighborhood to the suburbs so they don't have to be in fellowship with 'those people.'[15]

Thus, an adaptive church acknowledges and repents of collusion with corrupt powers that preserve inequity. Thinking of adaptation in evolutionary terms helps us see how the church has been infected with these harmful genes. It was the church that legitimated these harmful practices. Perhaps the greatest adaptation would be to discard this harmful DNA by seeking to make reparations, challenging unjust structures, and embodying real healing communities of shared power.

---

12. Leonardo Boff, *Ecclesiogenesis: The Base Communities Reinvent the Church* (Maryknoll, NY: Orbis, 1986) 25.

13. Day, *Religious Resistance to Neoliberalism*, 16.

14. Thurman, *Jesus and the Disinherited* (Boston: Beacon, 1996), 46.

15. Heath, *Mystic Way of Evangelism*, 63.

So how can adaptive ecclesiology help us preserve what is of God, but jettison the toxic, anti-God mutations of our DNA? More specifically, how do we bring this down to the ground floor of the local church?

The Toxic Loop

When churches get stuck in non-essential DNA they can become toxically, internally focused. In the attractional model, it is easy to get amnesia over the nature of our sentness, the very why of our existence. If this amnesia spreads throughout the congregation, one of the essential truths of our Christian faith can become toxic: "And they will call him Immanuel" (which means "God with us") (Matt 1:23).

This central claim can also cast a shadow. Whenever there is an "us" it always creates a "them." Whenever the focus is "I" it can exclude an "other." When all I can see is "me," I create an invisible "you." When we become so focused on God being with "us," the very inclusive nature of a community that invited sinners, tax-collectors, and sex-workers to the table is reversed. We become exclusive, as in God is only with "us." You can join "us," if you look like us, talk like us, and are the same age as us.

When a church has become fixated on this exclusive us-ness, then a toxic loop has been created. The toxic loop describes an often unconscious cycle of dysfunction, where a congregation has become entirely "us" fixated on excluding the "them." There is little to no dissatisfaction in this state. The only concern in this community is taking care of each other and preserving the status quo of a past that is no longer based in reality. It's like a walled city under siege. Imagine a museum that is owned by a group who would rather die staring at the exhibitions than sell tickets to let others inside.

Most churches decline and even die because the "us" of their "God with us" is too small. Rather than reflecting the divine dance of "making room" and mutual indwelling of the perichoresis of the Trinity, they become individualistic, isolated, and a closed system.

Process: The Möbius Strip— Breaking the Toxic Loop

Parker Palmer shares the analogy of the Möbius Strip in his book *A Hidden Wholeness: The Journey Toward an Undivided Life*. While the Möbius Strip is a concept that comes from mathematics, Palmer innovates this form to tangibly illustrate the journey of a healthy human soul. We want to push the analogy a bit further to describe the journey of a healthy church.

You could use a strip of paper, or simply take off your belt, to get a visual representation of this process. Palmer believes that we come into the world as an undivided whole but, over time, every person erects a wall between his or her inner and outer lives. One side of the strip represents the outer or onstage life, the "role" we play in creation. The concerns of the outer life are things like image, influence, and impact. The other side represents the inner or backstage life, the essence of who we are, or the "soul." This inner dimension reflects ideas, intuitions, feelings, values, and faith.[16]

Palmer suggests that the relational process embodied in the Möbius Strip occurs in four phases.

Stage One

In stage one, as newly minted human beings created in God's image, there is no separation between our inner and outer lives. In our earliest formative years of life, we are born whole, living in the fullness of life.

Stage Two

In stage two, we form a wall between our inner truth and our outer world. We form this wall largely to protect our inner vulnerabilities against external threats. As we develop, we learn that the world is a dangerous place, and that it is not safe to express our souls.

---

16.   Parker J. Palmer, *A Hidden Wholeness: The Journey Toward an Undivided Life: Welcoming the Soul and Weaving Community in a Wounded World* (San Francisco: Jossey-Bass, 2004), 32–49.

Stage Three

Stage three begins when living in a state of duplicity brings us to our knees. Trauma occurs in our inner or outer world, and we turn our wall into a circle. By bringing the two ends of our strip together we can see what some religious traditions have called centering. We center our lives on our inner truth and our core values. However, Palmer points out that this maneuver has a dark side. If we turn the circle horizontally, we can see that it now resembles a walled city or a gated community. We allow only certain people into this secret garden of withness while using the wall to keep unwanted visitors out; we limit the "us" by limiting access to our soul.

Stage Four

In the fourth and final stage, we break open that circle, twist one end of the strip, and reconnect the two ends together. The resulting form is called a Möbius Strip. If we use our finger to trace one side of the strip, we discover that, as we follow it, the inner world appears to express itself outward into the external world and vice versa. Now there is no longer an outside and an inside, but a continuous loop of co-creation in which the soul and the role are fully integrated. What is inside is always flowing out to affect the external world, and what is outside is always flowing back to affect what is within.

Awakening the Essential DNA

Now we want to add an innovation to Palmer's concept. We believe the Möbius Strip is a wonderful analogy for what is happening in the incarnation. Humanity had closed itself off from God, rejecting God's gracious offer of loving relationship. In putting on flesh, God breaks the closed loop and draws us into God's soul while simultaneously inviting us into God's role. God is constantly expanding God's withness and us-ness by inviting us into communion and a journey of co-creation.

The perichoretic nature of the Trinity helps us understand how God draws us into Godself, makes us "at-one," and fills and sends us out as ambassadors of God's withness and us-ness. So, the church has its origin in the sentness of Jesus, again "mission is the mother of theology," missiology and ecclesiology are one continuous loop of cocreation.

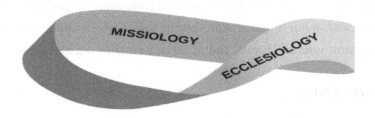

Now, apply the journey of the Möbius Strip to the journey that happens in the renewal and rebirth of a church. We have each served congregations that were in significant decline, some for many decades. The congregations had dwindled in number, and engagement with the community around them was little to non-existent. We find this analogy the most helpful in describing what actually happens or needs to happen for a church to reverse the process of decline.

Stage One

All churches are initially born in a state of wholeness. Every church that's ever been planted in any community is there to be "with" that community and expand the "us" of the new church. We have never heard of a church that was planted that didn't want to grow and reach new people. This is stage one in the soul journey Palmer describes. As a newly planted church there is no separation between its inner and outer lives. The church exists to be fully alive and expand the "withness and us-ness" that is the soul of the new organism.

Stage Two

In stage two, there is some kind of threat to the church, and thus we form a wall between the church's soul and its role in the community. Perhaps another church is planted across the street, or a major cultural shift occurs, or some kind of event triggers the community to protect itself. We form a wall in our impulse to protect the soul, to shelter inner vulnerabilities against external threats, and to create a tangible sense of belonging.

Stage Three

Stage three begins when we turn our wall into a circle. We center the community on inner truth and core values. However, the very wall we have created to protect the soul of the church prohibits the witness of God's presence in the community. While the wall may shelter against perceived threats, it also becomes a barrier to growth. The very divisiveness of the condition of the church creates an unhealthy paradigm and a survival mentality.

Rather than a community reaching out with the witness of God in neighborly love, self-preservation becomes the new normal. We protect the soul and the legacy of who we have always been. We have a well-defined "us." Typically, we only allow people who we perceive as safe to come into our circle. Again, the dark side of this maneuver is that our church now resembles a walled city or a gated community. We only allow people who look like us, believe like us, and have the same interests of self-preservation as us into the inner circle.

The "us" of our gated community diminishes until there is really no "us" left. Our withness is no longer extended to people outside the walls of the church building, but withness has now become about being with each other, and at any cost. The secret garden becomes a toxic place where nothing grows, the soul withers, and the "us" inevitably dies. In this condition, there is only one hope for this church.

Stage Four

In the fourth and final stage, a team of the willing must come and blow a hole in that wall. We must break open that circle by identifying or creating dissatisfaction, and when we do, usually a contingent of people will run out of the opening. They'll say things like, "We've never done it that way before," "We don't want to reach people like that," or "It's not safe in here anymore . . . the soul of our church has been exposed."

The task of breaking open that wall of dysfunction, then, is not easy or for the faint of heart. In adaptive leadership, this refers to orchestrating the conflict. Now, with the remnant inside the circle, the twist begins. We really don't like this part, no one likes being bent in new configurations. Human beings don't like change, but what we really fear is loss. In the disorientation, this is where exploration and sense-making become important.

Nevertheless, the shift continues, and the soul and role of the church are reconnected in a new configuration. Here is our Möbius Strip! In the new arrangement, we discover that the inner world of the church now appears to express out into the outer world in a continuous loop of co-creation. The soul of the church is constantly expressing out and affecting the surrounding community, and the community is constantly flowing back in to affect the inner world of the church. The distinction between outside and inside is no more. The form of the church is a fluid dance of making room for the other, one that reflects the perichoretic divine life of the Trinity.

This is not a "closed loop"; rather, we must understand this by means of a three-dimensional model. Through this loop of continuous co-creation, the withness and the us-ness of God are constantly expanding and contracting in a healthy cycle of full integration. What is inside is always flowing out to affect the world, and what is outside is always flowing back

19

to affect what is within. Think of it like a Velcro loop that is constantly engaging and bringing people in and out all the time.

Breaking the Wall

You might be asking, "So how do we break open the wall and bend into this new configuration of churches that have become gated communities?" In our experience, the only way that can happen is by creating an adaptative culture in those churches. We like to think of the words *apostolic, missional,* and *adaptive* as having deep resonance theologically. Yet these words may be like some dusty old books that were forgotten in the church's ancient library, but these words are integral to the history of every church that has ever existed. If you trace the history of a church back far enough, you will find a missional identity was once the soul. Apostolicity is a fundamental part of the church's DNA, and an apostolic church is always an adaptive church.

Fresh expressions catalyze renewal in existing congregations because they expand the "withness" and the "us-ness" of their communal life.

The focus of a fresh expression is not to revitalize an existing church, but rather to reach non-Christians in incarnational ways and form community with them in the normal rhythms and spaces of life. These are "fresh expressions" of that greater one, holy, apostolic, and catholic church, and a microcosm of that universal whole. However, fresh expressions do inadvertently revitalize existing churches in an adaptive process that resembles death and resurrection.

The breaking and twisting causes us to see and to ask, Who is our other? Some of the churches we served had existed in the same places since the mid-to-late-1800s, and yet the community just outside our walls didn't even know we were there.

Somehow, over time, in the life of every church and person, our "us" becomes too small. It is the central affirmation (essential DNA) of our Christian faith that we believe in one named Immanuel, "God with us."

The central claim is that God has somehow reached out and claimed our life with God's love, and that God is now with us, not above, or beyond, but "with."

As a sent community of God-withness, our central task is ever to expand the withness and us-ness of God in the world. It is an ever-widening circle of inclusive love. This is a very big "us" that includes all the people of the earth, persons of every tribe, caste, race, and political affiliation. We are called to reach others with the very same withness we have experienced in Christ. Every church is called to exist in this continual loop of co-creation, sharing in the life of the Trinity, laboring with God to draw all humanity into that communion.

Fresh expressions give us a way to rediscover core DNA and discard unhelpful or even harmful DNA. They break the loop and twist the congregation into a new shape. They reconfigure the congregation's orientation outward to the community again. The life of the church flows out into the community, the life of the community flows back into the church; these interactions release a trophic cascade of change in the larger communal ecosystem.

This can also happen in an inherited church. Audrey Warren led her congregation, First UMC in Miami, to flatten their existing building in order to partner with the community on a new and more relevant structure. For a father and his two sons, all architects, this was the only building they had ever designed together. Yet they gave their support for the greater purpose—the mission.

The Möbius Strip Exercise

Instructions: Prepare a strip of paper or use a belt (preferably with two sides) to create a Möbius Strip. Invite as many leaders as possible to join you for the exercise. Perhaps have a gathering around sharing food or a meal.

Step 1. Explain the stages of the Möbius Strip in a human life, from Parker Palmer's *A Hidden Wholeness*. One side of the strip is the soul, one side is the role.

Step 2. Explain how that process applies to the life of the church and the concept of the toxic loop.

Step 3. Ask the gathering to walk through the stages with you and identify those stages in the life of the church. Use the Möbius Strip as a visual aid as you walk through the stages.

Stage One: As a newly minted church created in the apostolic (sent) purpose, role and soul were one as the founders of our congregation sought to expand God's withness in our community. Can we recall our founding and core values?

Stage Two: Some threat occurred that caused our congregation to form a wall between our inner truth and our outer world. If we have experienced this stage, can we name the threat(s)?

Stage Three: Our wall begins to turn into a circle. We center the community on inner truth and core values. However, the very wall we have created to protect the soul of the church prohibits others from entering. Everyone starts to look the same; they are the same age, same race, and same class. Visitors don't seem to return, no matter how friendly we are. Are there signs that this is true for us?

Stage Four: Some brave team must break open the wall and twist the congregation's orientation outward. If this is where we are, how can we do this? Who will be the team responsible? Who is willing to speak about this to the congregation? Are we willing to accept the possibility of losing members? Who is willing to start planting fresh expressions in the community? Are you willing to serve on a team to that end?

CHAPTER THREE

Create

For if you have been cut from what is by nature a wild olive tree and grafted,
contrary to nature, into a cultivated olive tree, how much more will these natural
branches be grafted back into their own olive tree.
—Romans 11:24

Let's gather at the "tree of life." In terms of discerning essential DNA, discarding unhelpful and harmful DNA, and creating new arrangements, we find a helpful overarching metaphor in scripture.

The tree of life is a symbol of the continuity of God's plan for the renewal of the cosmos and one of the most consistent images of God's faithful presence. Our story starts at the tree (Gen 2:9), begins over at the tree on Golgotha (Gal 3:13) and continues eternally back at the tree in the urban garden of new creation (Rev 22:2).

This tree is the central image of an adaptive ecclesiology or a blended ecology. There is a life-giving exchange happening between the *inherited* church, with its rootedness and depth, and these new wild lifeforms, the *emerging* church. The hope here is to create a form of symbiosis. Stuart Murray, in *Church after Christendom* writes, "The brightest hope for the church after Christendom is a symbiotic relationship between inherited and emerging churches."[1]

In Romans 11, Paul speaks to the marvelous thing God has done in Jesus Christ, making Jews and Gentiles one living organism. He uses

---

1. Stuart Murray, *Church After Christendom* (Milton Keynes: Paternoster, 2004), 122.

the image of the olive tree as his central metaphor. Gentiles are the "wild branches" now *grafted* into the very same root system as the Jews. They are now one tree. A new creation organism has emerged through a process of grafting. As Paul says in Romans: "For if you have been cut from what is by nature a wild olive tree and grafted, contrary to nature, into a cultivated olive tree, how much more will these natural branches be grafted back into their own olive tree" (11:24).

In horticulture, grafting refers to a technique that leads to the formation of the graft union of the scion and rootstock. Genomic-scale mRNA is exchanged across graft junctions. This means that grafting leads to an exchange of genetic material between the scion and rootstock, resulting in the formation of a unique organism.

Thus, through this grafting process, there is an exchange at the fundamental level between the scion and the rootstock. The two species not only enter a symbiotic union, but they actually transform each other through an exchange of the foundational building blocks of their being. This is why we have advocated for the language of a "blended ecology."

For Paul, these diverse "species" of olive trees have been grafted together into one tree. The blended ecology way requires us to do some grafting to create new arrangements of the DNA.

The tree of life is for both Jew and Gentile alike; indeed, it is for all people. We will once again gather around this tree in the new creation. The church is a living composite organism of God's future breaking into the present. The deep roots of *inherited congregations* must be grafted together with the wild branches of the *emerging forms of church*, forming new creation ecosystems in our neighborhoods and networks.

Fresh expressions and other innovative ministries give us a vehicle to experiment with new arrangements of the DNA.

Alan Roxburgh says, "The temptation of many leaders remains the need to fix problems with big strategies, more programs, and importing programs from outside. Instead of defaulting to these predictable, manageable solutions that have the appearance of addressing challenges, create experiments around the edge."[2]

A fresh expression or other new innovative ministry forces a congregation to look outside itself. It provides a process to release this experimentation on the edge without giving up on the center. It breaks us open and reconfigures our soul in such a way that it touches our community again.

Fresh expressions don't just benefit the people that they reach, they transform the soul of existing congregations. They help us find a new metaphor and craft a new narrative. They catalyze dissatisfaction with the status quo by providing the stories that remind us who we are and what we are all about. They wake up local congregations from our apostolic amnesia, anchoring us in our core values. They provide a fresh vision of the future for congregations willing to take the road less traveled, the road of death and resurrection.

Planting fresh expressions of church in the community breaks the toxic loop. As you grow the inherited center, a small team that is sensitive to the dissatisfaction can begin the process of exploration on the edge, and journey into new possibilities.

Local congregations can think about changing DNA through pro-creation in the blended ecology way. We focus on the local church because it has the most significant potential to transform larger communal ecosystems as the "imperfect pilot plants of God's future world."[3] Every local church can be (re)mixed for mission, to reflect the conjunctive story of Temple and Tabernacle/Jerusalem and Antioch, deep roots and wild branches.

Tod Bolsinger's insight regarding the process of changing a church's DNA through giving birth is helpful here: "The new birth won't be all you or all them but a new creation, a new living culture that is a combination

2.   Alan J. Roxburgh, *Missional: Joining God in the Neighborhood* (Grand Rapids, MI: Baker, 2011), 176.

3.   Graham Cray, et al., *Fresh Expressions of Church and the Kingdom of God* (Norwich, UK: Canterbury, 2012), 18.

of the past and the future that you represent."[4] Cultivating new things reconfigures the existing church in a new way. *Emergence* occurs as the new whole can no longer be reduced to the smaller parts; the parts have blended together in a novel resurrection form. The reconfigured organism is now constantly reproducing.

We now have some recycling work before us. It is the work of stone rolling and burial cloth unraveling. This is resurrection work. This is a mix of old and new to create what can be. However, the more apt description of what we are doing is futurefitting. We are taking the inherited mode of church and fitting it with fresh, new, green ecclesiology to cultivate a sustainable future. We tend, fertilize, trim, and care for the existing tree and go out and cast the seeds, grafting the new life together in a wonderful new compact organism.

---

4. Ted E. Bolsinger, *Canoeing the Mountains: Christian Leadership in Uncharted Territory* (Downers Grove, IL: IVP, 2016), 82.

CHAPTER FOUR

Start Small

Therefore do not worry about tomorrow, for tomorrow will worry about itself.
Each day has enough trouble of its own.
—Matthew 6:34

Stop asking God to bless what you're doing. Find out what God's doing.
It's already blessed.
—Bono

The first duty of love is to listen.
—Paul Tillich

We appreciate the recovery community's commitment to "live one day at a time." This idea of being present, not stuck with our heads in the past, or worried about what might come tomorrow is drawn from the teaching of Jesus himself: "Do not worry about tomorrow, each day has enough trouble of its own" (Matt 6:34).

We believe this is a key mindset for adaptive ecclesiology. We have spent a great deal of time and resources in long-range planning, often with a frustration in the outcomes. The adaptive mindset employs a short-term, iterative, experimental approach, or "effectual reasoning."

Michael recently arrived at a new congregation during the pandemic, St. Marks UMC in Ocala, Florida. About twelve faithful members were all that remained. Together, they held a community-listening session. They sent out fliers and did social media promotion, inviting the community to join the session. They asked attendees what the main challenges and opportunities in the neighborhood were. One issue that arose was food insecurity. One of the attendees was Pastor Betti Jefferson, a black church planter who was distributing weekly truckloads of food in a vacant lot nearby.

Pastor Betti and St. Marks UMC combined forces, offering a dedicated space for her church plant, refrigeration for the food items, and a distribution location for the hundreds of people who came each week.

From this, the team developed a vision for a dinner church. They would gather on Wednesday nights for a community dinner, prayer, and Jesus stories. The faithful church folks, all of them chronologically gifted, protested their ability to make a dinner once a week. Michael suggested that they try the experiment for three months, with two people working together in teams to cook the meal each week so the burden was shared.

Each week, the team began to invite participants to help cook, clean up, and provide the Jesus stories. Many were excited just to make a contribution. Attendees formed relationships with the inherited church members as they served together. Within three months about forty regular attendees came each week and were sharing the load of putting on the dinner. Today, the twelve faithful show up each week, not to work, but to gather around the tables to eat with their new friends. They went from serving to being served, and now a spirit of joy permeates this new emerging faith community.

Small experiments. Short-term thinking. Empowerment. Partnerships. Shared leadership. This is essential to the adaptive way.

The phenomenon of trophic cascades mentioned earlier is about the cumulative impact of relatively small changes in a given ecosystem. Small Changes = Massive Impact over time.

The key to cultivating new ecosystems, is "dream big, start small." This process is all about small, continuous, disruptive changes. You are a keystone species in the ecosystem of your community. The new environment we are seeking to cultivate in a revitalization context is the blended ecology. Let's return to the foundational image: a tree thriving in the desert, and in its shade is the tapestry of color, new flowers, and life forms thriving in the root system.

This is a garden of innovation amidst a barren death-dealing context. The blended organisms are giving life to each other in a symbiotic relationship as fresh life, fresh oxygen, and fresh spaces are being generated.

The blended ecology is not created through a single act of massive change. It does not take shape by uprooting the existing tree or chopping it up into firewood. In fact, there are three major areas to focus on activity to produce the new blended ecosystem:

1. caring, trimming, and fertilizing the existing tree;
2. planting, cultivating, and fertilizing the fresh life forms;
3. grafting the old and new life forms together.

These are small changes, but with massive implications for the ecosystem. The tree will die without appropriate care. If the tree dies, the new life forms cannot exist without its shade and the nutrients of the complex root system. For the ecosystem engineers, this is a delicate balance. We must think process; thus, adaptation is best understood more in the organic language of trophic cascades than in referring to programs or products.

While competence in organizational leadership is necessary, what is imperative is combining it with relational and adaptive leadership skills. The ecosystem is a complex network of life; there are extraneous variables that cannot be anticipated or at times even measured. When the wolves were introduced back in Yellowstone, no one could have anticipated the massive impact: the growth of trees, a renewed abundance of life forms, the reshaping of the environment itself, and the changing of the rivers.

When cultivating a new ecosystem, it is essential to remember Paul's words: "I planted the seed, Apollos watered it, but God has provided the growth" (1 Cor 3:6). The only one who really has the power to bring dead things back to life is God. We can do everything in our power, but in revitalization, we are completely reliant upon God's power. Fortunately, God creates new ecosystems through the process of the trophic cascades.

The phenomenon of the Trophic Cascade permeates scripture. God uses small voices, small people, and small beginnings to unleash the power of resurrection and transform the universe. Small acts of love have massive kingdom potential to create new ecosystems. "Cups of cold water" create trophic cascades, that in the new creation, the ecosystem becomes the river of life (Matt 10:40-42; Rev 21). Ecosystems become sick when artificial conditions are forced upon them. Ecosystems become toxic when they are polluted. God is all about (re)creating new ecosystems.

These small acts must be embodied in our daily living. It takes the kind of patience, consistency, vision, and proactive thinking we discussed earlier, and which Alan Kreider describes as the "patient ferment." Kreider brings out in a remarkable way the early mission strategy of the primitive church: patience. The early church was not the attractional model, in the modern sense. They had no program of evangelism, no street corner preaching, no buildings to attract people.[1]

In fact, during times of imperial persecution, any of those activities could get you killed.

It was how the first Christians lived the way of Jesus that God used to grow the church from an oppressed minority among the religious diversity of the Roman Empire, to such a massive population of people, Emperor Constantine officially adopted the movement as the state religion. The primary form of evangelism was the consistent behavior patterns of those first Christians, the instinctual rhythms of their relational being. The lives of these people were the "attraction" to outsiders—not buildings, rituals, or forceful oratory demonstrations.[2]

These holy habits are the means of grace, the works of piety, and the works of justice and mercy working together.

The early church was a blended ecology, but the primary mode was emerging. The church scattered, with a few centers where the gathered model was a reality. This is adaptive ecclesiology.

---

1. Alan Kreider, *The Patient Ferment of the Early Church: The Improbable Rise of Christianity in the Roman Empire* (Grand Rapids, MI: Baker, 2016), 9.

2. Kreider, *The Patient Ferment of the Early Church*, 39–40.

We find ourselves on a new frontier where the emerging, missional, scattered model is most appropriate for reaching new people. Most people from upcoming generations in our post-everything context are not going to show up at our steeples and cathedrals on a Sunday morning. No matter how compelling our preaching, no matter how awesome our music, no matter how pristine our buildings, the largest demographic of our population is simply not going to show up. How do we release the keystone species to catalyze trophic cascades in our communal ecosystems? How can local churches transform the larger ecosystem and provide places where people can be released into the flows of a networked society?

Starting from the Center— Living on the Edge

In adaptive ecclesiology, there are primarily two places we must focus our attention: the *center* and the *edge*. Tree and seedlings. Deep roots, wild branches. Jerusalem and Antioch. Let's consider the center the inherited congregation and systems, and the edge the fresh expressions of church or other missional experiments. We need to split our time, energy, and resources equally between those two focus areas, with fresh expressions offering us a way to do the latter effectively. However, we must start with the inherited congregation (from "Jerusalem and in all Judea and Samaria, and to the ends of the earth"). If the center is not healthy, the whole ecosystem suffers.

Graham Cray reminds us that an apostolic call is not always concerning a new geographic location, but a fresh way of engaging within the same parish.[3] The fresh expressions approach provides a powerful vehicle for the (re)missioning of inherited congregations. Thus, our starting point is the people in the inherited congregation.

---

3. Graham Cray, et al., *Fresh Expressions of Church and the Kingdom of God* (Norwich: Canterbury, 2012), 20.

Tod Bolsinger writes, "unless we demonstrate that we are credible on the map, no one is going to follow us off the map."[4] Before any transformational work can begin, the community of leaders needs to cultivate a healthy environment for "aligned shared values to guide all decision making."[5] Indeed, identifying these shared values undergirds the shaping of a congregation for mission.[6]

Because of the complexity of cultivating new ecosystems from declining congregations, the guiding principle is simplicity: stripping down inherited church systems to their simplest forms. The inherited church most likely has years of accumulated vision statements, strategic goal documents, and internal protocols. While we don't need to do away with those, we do need to go on a journey that takes us back to first principles, "a desire to reach behind the present tradition to the values which give it life and meaning for today."[7]

While we must start at the tree in the inherited center, we must hold this in tension with the reality that for many churches no amount of activity there will birth renewal. We can love God, love each other, and still close. We need to love the neighborhoods and networks of our community as well. Most revitalization strategies fail because they never get out of Jerusalem; we need to get to Antioch.

Quality Care and Disruptive Innovation Departments

To approach this in a practical way, think of your church as having primarily two departments, or better yet, as having two teams: quality care (the center) and disruptive innovation (the edge).

---

4. Tod E. Bolsinger, *Canoeing the Mountains: Christian Leadership in Uncharted Territory* (Downers Grove, IL: IVP, 2018), 50.

5. Bolsinger, *Canoeing the Mountains*, 79.

6. Paul Bayes, et al., *Mission-Shaped Parish: Traditional Church in a Changing World* (New York: Seabury, 2010), 3.

7. Steven J. Croft, *Mission-Shaped Questions: Defining Issues for Today's Church* (New York: Seabury, 2010), 196.

Dave Ferguson highlights the danger of creating an "R&D Department" in local churches. We hear his wisdom about attempting quick-fix solutions and creating silos where missional engagement is done by one "department" of the church. We also agree with his passionate call for the entire church to be engaged missionally.[8] However, our experience has been that this is not realistic in most inherited congregations. It is much easier to do in a church plant when it is built into the DNA from the beginning. In the inherited congregation, an apostolic awakening must take place first.

Cultivating the blended ecology in local congregations is about embracing the concept of Jerusalem and Antioch. While most of the committees, teams, and meetings will be focused on quality care (Jerusalem), identifying some of your key leaders to start a new department is a simple change that can have a massive impact. This is your "Antioch team." These are the folks you want to collaborate with through exploring improvisation and experimentation.

As Tod Bolsinger says, "experimental innovations are the key to surviving in a changing world."[9] This gives every church an opportunity to create a disruptive innovation division within the inherited system.

Resurrection is a remix, the power of God to take what is and reconfigure it in a splendid new creation. For churches to adapt we are going to need a remix of our current structure.

Jesus speaks of the value of both old and new wineskins: "new wine is put into fresh wineskins, and so both are preserved" (Matt 9:17). Wineskins are merely structures that support the fermentation and delivery of wine. Structures matter, and when they are flexible, they can support growth and release life. When they are overly rigid, they can be confining and even suffocating. Our structures flow from our legitimating narrative, which is inextricably linked with the person at the center of our story. The form from which the church is derived is the Trinity. The blended ecology

---

8. Alan Hirsch and Dave Ferguson, *On the Verge: A Journey into the Apostolic Future of the Church* (Grand Rapids, MI: Zondervan, 2011), 236.

9. Bolsinger, *Canoeing the Mountains*, 126.

resembles the dynamic relational interplay of perichoresis. The church is shaped to facilitate the fermentation and delivery of the vintage and fresh forms of God's new creation love in the world.

It is dangerous when we make structures a power unto themselves. Phil Potter, in speaking to pioneering a new future for declining congregations, writes: "Structures have a powerful influence, and the source of that power can be the key to life or bring the kiss of death."[10] "We've always done it that way before" can become a form of idolatry.

Existing congregations restructured by adaptive ecclesiology can join the disruptive power of the Spirit. Innovation is released through experimentation, and shared leadership is dispersed in dispersed, polycentric, forms. In discussing a missional ministry for a missional church, Alan Hirsh reveals that the breakdown often occurs at a structural level because people are unwilling "to reconfigure ministry to suit the missional context."[11]

Restructuring in this way is hard, but one of the reasons many churches fail is they try to change too much too fast. It's incredibly difficult to restructure an inherited congregation entirely. The good news about adaptive ecclesiology . . . is that you don't have to.

This analogy is helpful as we find ourselves to be in the midst of a paradigm shift, where we are thinking and working between two ages, even between two ways of understanding the universe. A world where the rationalized efficiency, professional management, and bureaucratic structures of twentieth-century corporations exist beside the mash-up, the blockchain, and the collective super-intelligence of Google. It is a world of neighborhoods and networks. Our inherited church systems are still functioning largely in the mechanistic Newtonian framework, while fresh expressions allow us to integrate advancements from the new science into our communal life. Adaptive leadership harnesses the power of our

---

10. Phil Potter, *Pioneering a New Future: A Guide to Shaping Change and Changing the Shape of Church* (Abingdon, UK: Bible Reading Fellowship, 2015), 151.

11. Alan Hirsch, et al., *The Permanent Revolution: Apostolic Imagination and Practice for the 21st Century Church* (San Francisco: Jossey-Bass, 2012), 7.

current in-betweenness by making some additions to the existing system, not starting over from scratch.

Setting up small experiments connected to the inherited system can open positive feedback loops.12 In overly stable systems, we need to establish kinds of onsite laboratories where small changes can occur through experimentation that will eventually feed back into the system.

Sometimes the dissatisfaction we seek to avoid is at the heart of the adaptive challenge. Consider how dissatisfaction can be used positively to catalyze a process of transformation.

Dissatisfaction— Look for the Dying Cows

In *The Innovators Way: Essential Practices for Successful Innovation*, Denning and Dunham share the story of Louis Pasteur, arguably one of the greatest innovators in history. In the 1870s, when cow and sheep populations were being decimated by a strange disease that threatened to destabilize the economic stability of France, Pasteur was called in to work on the problem. He had already previously shown how to prevent wine from spoiling (he invented the process that now bears his name pasteurization) and saved the silk industry by identifying the microbe that caused the decimation of French silkworms.[13]

Pasteur had a unique method: he took his laboratory to the site of a major problem out in the field. He produced a series of major innovations in this way in the wine, dairy, silk, and chicken industries. In the case of cows, he studied how the animals were getting sick onsite and, through his discovery, saved the sheep and cattle industries. One lesson here, according to Denning and Dunham, is to "look for the dying cows."[14]

12. Michael Moynagh, *Church in Life: Emergence, Ecclesiology and Entrepreneurship* (London: SCM, 2017), 33.

13. Peter J. Denning and Robert Dunham, *The Innovator's Way: Essential Practices for Successful Innovation* (Cambridge, MA: MIT, 2010), xxiii.

14. Denning and Dunham, *The Innovator's Way*, xxiv.

For a community facing an adaptive challenge, someone has to plug into what people value and show them how to make their cows healthy again. Often people will not adopt a new way of thinking or being unless they experience great dissatisfaction first. Unfortunately, folks are most receptive to change only amid a major breakdown. Part of this process is helping people acknowledge that dissatisfaction and demonstrating great value in adopting the new way.

Pasteur's method of bringing his laboratory to the site of a major problem helped him discern the problem from a position of withness. His perspective was from within the problem, not removed from it in some ivory tower. His solutions were improvisational. In the case of the dying cows and sheep, through experimentation, he discovered the cause was a microorganism. He devised a way to control the microorganism, then he conducted a dramatic experiment to demonstrate his solution. Pasteur attracted powerful allies to his experiments, who supported his science, enabling his discoveries to amplify throughout the whole system.[15]

Ecclesial innovation begins with a group of people experiencing dissatisfaction, being willing to explore, and engaging in sense-making at the site of the emerging decline scenario. There, onsite, they can experiment as they start exploring together, in an improvisational way, the new possibilities the Spirit is breathing forth. With the tree, (the inherited congregation) as our base of operations, we need to make spaces in the shade where we can experiment, plant new organisms, and then see what happens (the fresh expressions).

From this experimentation, new ideas and developments arise that have the potential to spread throughout the entire system. This can lead a community to the edge of chaos, and potentially to a new state of self-organization.

The *edge of chaos* in the journey of innovation refers to the sweet spot between enough openness to release change, and enough structure to sustain order. Overly stable systems suffocate innovation; conversely, too

---

15. Denning and Dunham, *The Innovator's Way*, xxv.

much rapid change can destroy systems. Theologically, this is about the liminal space between creation and new creation, it is about opening ourselves to the Spirit bringing forth a new future while balancing this with the Spirit's activity in the past.[16]

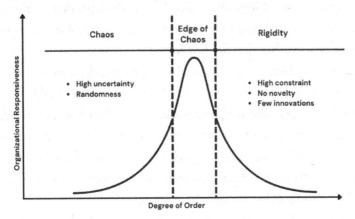

The community, through a series of conversations, receives feedback that can catalyze change in new directions. Consider the example of St. Mark's in Ocala choosing to start a small community dinner experiment. They started to see value in the effects of this "experiment," and how it could open the potential of a new future. Now the Wednesday night dinner church is a major aspect of congregational life.

Allowing for these small changes out in the yard beneath the tree, so to speak, begins to transform the ecosystem through synergistic interactions. In complexity thinking, the term *attractor* describes the potential for change.

An *attractor* refers to a system's direction of travel, or to the specific subset of states that a social system may take, which corresponds to its normal behavior toward which it will naturally gravitate. Social systems are organized around these attractors: ideas and practices that have gained support.

16. Moynagh, *Church in Life*, 34.

The transformation of a system occurs when a "strange attractor" gathers enough support to challenge successfully the existing pattern of an organization. New attractors destabilize the system, and a kind of tug of war can then occur between old and new. While operating within a certain region of possibility, determined by path dependency (the past of an organization directing its future possibilities), a multitude of paths becomes possible within that defined region.[17]

Creating a small team, the disruptive innovation department, specifically focused on the work of cultivating fresh expressions, could become an on-site laboratory. The fresh expressions they plant becomes the new attractor that can draw the entire system in a new direction. Through feedback loops (what we consider *grafting* in our larger metaphor), the small changes that emerge from this team's experimentation have infinite potential to transform the communal ecosystem.

This helps us discover the value of both radical and incremental progress, to which we now turn.

---

17. Moynagh, *Church in Life*, 24.

CHAPTER FIVE

Innovate Two Ways

Neither is new wine put into old wineskins; otherwise, the skins burst,
and the wine is spilled, and the skins are ruined, but new wine is put into
fresh wineskins, and so both are preserved.
—Matthew 9:17 *(Emphasis added)*

We believe that adaptive leadership must employ both radical and incremental progress simultaneously. A radical innovation, also called disruptive innovation, can be a significant breakthrough in the form of a new model, technology, process, or concept that disrupts the existing status quo. Incremental innovation, by comparison, refers to a significant improvement or upgrade to the performance or functionality of an existing model, service, technology, or process.

While incremental progress is usually the way of the center (Jerusalem), radical progress is often located out on the edge (Antioch). The former involves helping inherited congregational life flourish in new ways. The latter can include joining Jesus in the cultivation of incarnational communities in the flows of a networked, mobile, post-everything, hyperconnected world.

As we cultivate ecosystems in the manner Jesus reveals, we must learn to see the places where we live as "very good." God is like a master who has planted good seeds in God's garden (Matt 13:24-30). Goodness, beauty, and truth are baked into the cosmos at every layer. We reject the assumptions of the imminent frame and the false dichotomy of sacred and secular. We understand that God is already at work in the world, and we begin to discern how we might join in on what God is up to. God is good. People are good. Communities are good.

We can hold this together in dialectical tension with the obvious pollution and fragmentation that exist in our communities. People appear separated from their lives with God and each other. It's like poisonous weeds are growing in the garden as well and, as Jesus informs us, "an enemy has done this" (Matt 13:24-30). The infectious weeds cause fragmentation and they isolate us from our neighbors.

As Guder and Barrett write in *Missional Church*: "In a hyper-connected world, yet trapped in the individualism of the modern condition, we are alone."[1] Longing for real community and connection in a network society typified by disconnection from one's locality made possible in 5G speed by flows in virtual, cultural, and physical globalization. The deepest pain of our human condition is isolation.

It is in this aching condition of isolation that the church has a gift to offer. In fact, the church alone can give the greatest gift of all—communal life with Jesus. This is a gift the world desperately needs. This is a community of unconditional love centered around the risen Christ, where true authenticity can take place and loneliness can be healed.

Urbanization has been a trend leading to massive social restructuring, the transformation toward a network society. Cities' massive growth also translates to more concentrated areas of pollution.

Some of our best minds are working on retrofitting cities with green spaces, to offer fresh air and heal the places where we do life. Numerous studies have demonstrated that access to green spaces, such as parks and recreational areas, is associated with improved overall health and reduced morbidity and mortality.[2]

---

1. Darrell L. Guder and Lois Barrett, *Missional Church: A Vision for the Sending of the Church in North America* (Grand Rapids, MI: Eerdmans, 1998), 43.

2. Extensive research done by the World Health Organization can be summarized here: "Urban Green Spaces and Health," www.euro.who.int/__data/assets/pdf_file/0005/321971/Urban-green-spaces -and-health-review-evidence.pdf?ua=1.

Green spaces are places that not only offer fresh oxygen amid thick urban air, but real community. People gather in these green spaces, connecting by flows around shared practices. They exercise, connect with one another, and disconnect from the frantic workcycle. Green spaces allow people to heal from their chronic fatigue and exhaustion. Thus, people gather in these green spaces for friendship, which increases quality of life—not just environmentally but relationally.

Retrofitting cities is an example of incremental progress.

An example of radical progress would be the construction of entirely new eco-cities, like Masdar City. Masdar is a sustainable urban desert settlement in Abu Dhabi, United Arab Emirates. It is humanity's first attempt to build a zero-carbon emissions city. It's a free zone, designed to be a business hub and a destination for cleantech companies.

In many parts of the United States, the United Kingdom, and Europe, the critical challenge leans more toward dealing with aging building materials and unsustainable urban infrastructure. In the United Kingdom alone, the already-built environment accounts for over two-thirds of total carbon emissions, and less than 1 to 2 percent of total building stock each year is new construction. Around 70 percent of the total 2010 building stock will still be in use in 2050.[3]

Just as building new eco-cities alone will not save the planet's declining health, simply planting new faith communities will not stop the church's decline. Existing cities are, in fact, the source of the most pressing environmental pollution and resource depletion problems. Just as existing congregations are, in fact, contributing to the church's decline.

Retrofitting current cities is the most important task for healing our ecosystem and enabling human thriving in the future. We need incremental and radical progress working toward the remixing of neighborhoods in a sustainable way and creating green spaces. This is also the church's greatest challenge today. While we need to continue with Masdar City-like

---

3. Malcom Eames, et al., "Retrofit 2050: Critical Challenges for Urban Transitions," accessed October 2017, http://centaur.reading.ac.uk/36187/1/critical%20challenges%20briefing-March%202014.pdf.

church plants, we need to make futurefitting existing congregations for sustainability a main feature of our work.

The church can be involved in the planting of green spaces in the community . . . literally. We believe in a good creator God, who created a "very good" universe that reflects God's being. So, if we believe that humanity, as reflections of God, is called to steward the earth, we should be leading the way in planet care initiatives. We should be offering interpretive leadership, proclaiming a counternarrative to a growing population of humanity that is literally poisoning the planet with our lifestyles.

However, in fresh expressions we use the concept of green space as a figuration for the first-, second-, and third-places within our larger communal ecosystems. This helps us envision cultivating a blended ecology in our community. The world that is our parish, is a complex web of life, relationships, and interacting habitats. Within the larger ecosystem we will need to employ both radical and incremental innovation.

Planting fresh expressions of church is like futurefitting our communities with green spaces that heal both the communal environment and the isolation of individual, fragmented souls.

While we are using cities primarily as an illustration here, we want to note how fresh expressions show great potential with rural churches. Michael has written a guide for this in *Fresh Expressions of the Rural Church*. Among the shifts of globalization and urbanization, many local churches continue to exist in rural contexts.

Yet, to understand the size and speed of the urbanization shift, some facts and figures are important: in 1800, only 3 percent lived in urban areas; by 1900, that number grew to 14 percent; and in the last ten years, over half of the global population now lives in urban areas, with projections as high as 61 percent by 2025.[4]

This is creating a crisis for rural churches, as population decreases translate to continued congregational decline. Rural churches may be

---

4.   J. R. Woodward, *Creating a Missional Culture: Equipping the Church for the Sake of the World* (Downers Grove, IL: IVP, 2012), 72.

able to see their communities as larger ecosystems, and their edge may be planting fresh expressions in more populated areas nearby. When the neighborhood is minimal, a rural church can harness the power of networks. While the people we reach there may never attend our "missional hub," this creates a way for us to be the church with them.

The rural congregation can become the homebase sending point for the ordinary heroes of the priesthood of believers. Also, rural congregations have the advantage of potentially being the only "third-place" in the community. Shier-Jones, speaking of the value of fresh expressions meeting on a church campus, writes that "the local church is the only landlord with rooms to let at reasonable rents, with all the facilities and resources needed to host a small experimental gathering."[5] In a rural or small-town context, the church may be the only space available to gather for events. Furthermore, throughout the United Kingdom, small, rural congregations cultivating fresh expressions are taking on different forms of revitalization as well.[6]

The process of cultivating fresh expressions, while holding that together with grafting them into the inherited congregation, is the blended ecology way. This allows us to employ both radical and incremental progress, as we live one day at a time. This is an adaptive journey in which we balance an openness to novelty while maintaining integrity within the inherited system.

We want to suggest two distinct frameworks for incremental and radical innovation. The next two chapters will explore them in depth.

---

5. Angela Shier-Jones, *Pioneer Ministry and Fresh Expressions of Church* (London: SPCK, 2009), 95.

6. Sally Gaze, *Mission-Shaped and Rural: Growing Churches in the Countryside* (London: Church House, 2006), xviii.

CHAPTER SIX

A Framework for Incremental Innovation

And he who was seated on the throne said,
"Behold, I am making all things new."
—Revelation 21:5

As we explore a simple framework for innovation it's important to clarify what innovation actually is. Innovation is not simply about invention, creating a new thing, or generating a new idea. Innovation is not the answer to the problem of church decline.

Innovation is commonly understood as applying our ingenuity and skills to create our way out of a problem. "Disruptive innovation" can also merely be creative destruction under a fancier name. Talk of "innovation" often falls into the trap of "all new things" coming out of the consumeristic cult of "brand spanking new" and "new and improved," rather than the biblical way of Jesus and the promise of God "making all things new." Further, the crisis facing the church is not to become "relevant" through innovation in a post-Christendom reality. Communal life in Jesus cannot be irrelevant when we truly get a taste of it. This is another false assumption, and fresh expressions are not intended to make church relevant. The true way of Christian innovation is a pathway of death and resurrection, and it is a road less traveled.

Michael has written at length in *Deep and Wild* and *Fresh Expressions in a Digital Age* about "the innovator's dilemma." In the declining systems of the church this refers to the position clergy and their teams now find themselves in: the challenge of discerning whether to devote energy to sustaining the established organization or unleashing innovation to create something new.

In these two works, Michael tried to show this is a false either/or proposition and that "dual transformation" flips the dilemma. Every congregation must both "grow the center and experiment on the edge" simultaneously.

True innovators help communities adopt new ways and create cultural change.[1] They help people begin to use an invention, adopt a practice, or embrace a new way. Adventures are wired in the Spirit for innovation; it's their primary gifting. The community's adoption of what the team of adventurers initiates becomes the "new normal" of their way of life.

Is there a simple framework that can help us embody Christian innovation?

We will be using emerging insight from the new science and *Church in Life: Emergence, Ecclesiology and Entrepreneurship*. Michael Moynagh most brilliantly explores fresh expressions as a form of ecclesial emergence. Using sources primarily from complexity thinking and effectuation theory, Moynagh creates an innovation framework.[2] This framework will be a guide for ecclesial innovation.

This involves the journey of dissatisfaction, exploration, sense-making, amplification, and reaching the edge of chaos, which leads to transformation. The community itself lives out and sustains this transformation, a form of emergence or resurrection.

---

1. Peter J. Denning and Robert Dunham, *The Innovator's Way: Essential Practices for Successful Innovation* (Cambridge, MA: MIT, 2010), xiii.

2. Michael Moynagh, *Church in Life: Emergence, Ecclesiology and Entrepreneurship* (London: SCM, 2017), 11.

45

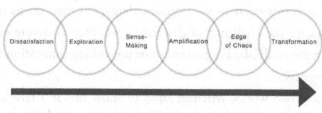

underpinned by prayer, on-going listening, and relationships with the wider church

1. Dissatisfaction: This is the initial disequilibrium or instability that must occur in a system in order to release innovation. Moynagh describes this, theologically speaking, as the gap between the present and God's future, or between the current realities and the promised kingdom. This is "prophetic dissatisfaction."[3] The main idea here is that the perspective of "we've always done it like this" is no longer healthy or effective. Embracing, and even catalyzing, dissatisfaction allows for adapting to a new context to occur.

2. Exploration: This is the process of the community reflecting upon its current experience and releasing experimentation. In response to dissatisfaction, old norms and assumptions are challenged, driving improvisation. Moynagh refers to this as a "Spirit-led process of trial and error, which is a means of discerning God's rule."[4] Essentially, this resembles making it up as you go along. It's the design thinking concept of failing-forward, iterating, trying something, then interpreting the results. Rather than creating a plan and trying to implement it (causal reasoning), this is exploring truth as it emerges through action (effectual reasoning).

3. Sense-Making: This has to do with helping the organization understand what it's experiencing. This is a shift in our Western understanding of leadership. Rather than emphasizing the individual effort of a particular

---

3. Moynagh, *Church in Life*, 29.

4. Moynagh, *Church in Life*, 31.

person "leading the change," a community of leaders enters a process of discernment to interpret the emerging realities. During the change, various leaders in the community help a group create a new narrative, one that is tethered to the historic identity of the community but is also responding to the Spirit's activity now.

4. Amplification: This refers to the process through which the Spirit multiplies and expands small changes through positive feedback.[5] New ideas and practices start to go viral within the community. Feedback can be both verbal and action-oriented, as people describe and respond to the change. These small changes begin to restructure the communal organization as a whole.

5. Reaching the Edge of Chaos: Systems that are excessively stable dampen innovation. As Moynagh says, being on the "edge of chaos is about being open to what the Spirit is bringing from the future, while building on what the Spirit has done in the past . . . Hope and history rhyme."[6] Instability is a sign of openness to change. However, too much change can tear the system apart. This process refers to the balance between an openness to novelty and faithfulness to a community's identity.

6. Transformation: This is the end result of the previous five processes. It occurs when bottom-up, self-organizing change leads to the creation of a remixed organism. The new organism retains the same DNA but is transfigured in new ways. The greater whole can no longer be reduced to the sum of its parts. Through a series of synergistic interactions, the Spirit has birthed a new creation, a resurrection community. To use a more organizationally friendly term, the transformation could be considered a form of *revitalization*.

While these six processes are not sequential stages—but rather co-evolving phenomena—it's more helpful to explore them in this order.

We began this journey with the prophet Jeremiah, so let's utilize his leadership as a demonstration of the incremental innovation framework.

---

5. Moynagh, *Church in Life*, 33.

6. Moynagh, *Church in Life*, 34.

Jeremiah models interpretive leadership for us. The religious and political systems of Jeremiah's day lived in a "lifeworld" that was an artificial ecosystem. They had made false assumptions that shaped their behavioral patterns. Those who inhabited the positions of authority in Jeremiah's day consisted of the royal household, the priests, and the court prophets. They interpreted scripture and their greater ecosystem in clearly defined ways.

Jeremiah confronted their assumptions and presented a shocking counternarrative. He challenged the current systems with both his voice and his embodied actions.

Jeremiah adopted several very unpopular prophetic stances, including advising against aligning politically with Egypt; condemning the use of slaves in building projects; proclaiming that God was using Nebuchadnezzar to humble the people; presenting the destruction of Jerusalem as God's will; and, then, once captivity and exile had taken place, suggesting that it would be a long-term scenario.

Jeremiah would not be the pastor most congregations received with open arms. This would essentially be like someone coming to a church and saying, "God's going to tear this nation and this church apart, we will go into exile and stay for a long time." As you can imagine, this would not be a very popular posture to take! Jeremiah wouldn't last long in most US churches today.

Jeremiah is guiding the people through a process that looks like this, the innovation framework:

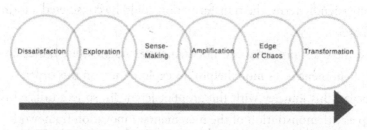

underpinned by prayer, on-going listening, and relationships with the wider church

In captivity, the community had moved fully into a state of *dissatisfaction*. Yet, even in that state, the other prophets of Jeremiah's day sought to comfort that dissatisfaction with a promise of a swift return. In the midst of this dissatisfaction, *Jeremiah leads the community of interpreters to create a new narrative through exploration and sense-making.*

In the innovation journey, he is helping the community through the process of *exploration*. He is also helping them reflect upon their current experience and consider experimenting with new possibilities. In their dissatisfaction, old norms and assumptions are challenged, opening the possibility of innovation.

Jeremiah's most pronounced counternarrative may have powerful application for the church today:

> Thus says the Lord of hosts, the God of Israel, to all the exiles whom I have sent into exile from Jerusalem to Babylon: Build houses and live in them; plant gardens and eat what they produce. Take wives and have sons and daughters; take wives for your sons, and give your daughters in marriage, that they may bear sons and daughters; multiply there, and do not decrease. But seek the welfare of the city where I have sent you into exile, and pray to the Lord on its behalf, for in its welfare you will find your welfare. For thus says the Lord of hosts, the God of Israel: Do not let the prophets and the diviners who are among you deceive you, and do not listen to the dreams that they dream, for it is a lie that they are prophesying to you in my name; I did not send them, says the Lord. (Jer 29:4-9)

The people are called to embrace a new social imaginary in which not only are they called to accept their exile, but also to establish themselves in this context as their new home! The community must now adapt and reflect upon its current experience, and the loss of old norms and assumptions are challenged.

Jeremiah, through experimentation and improvisation, is guiding the community through the process of *sense-making* as it explores what fidelity to God may look like amid the emergent scenario. The people begin iterating new forms of community and interpreting the results. This is not a causal process, that of developing strategic steps toward some predefined goal. Rather, it is an effectual process that explores truth as it emerges through acting within the new scenario. Jeremiah encourages both allegiance to God's action in the community's past and encourages a series of experiments toward a new future.

We are moving more fully into the reality of a network society, a kind of exile for the inherited church, and we won't be going back any time soon.

In many churches there is a false optimism that everything will be fine; some are saying, "Let's just wait, things will change." Some think we just need to tweak what we are currently doing, do it bigger and better, pray harder, and fast for longer periods. Jeremiah was confronting the fact that spiritual disciplines like fasting were not mechanisms to make God do what we want. Instead, they were spiritual practices that sustained us during adversity and pain, as we sang the songs of Zion in a foreign land. Continuing in the attractional model alone and doing things the way we've always done them before is not going to awaken the church.

In the innovative framework, Jeremiah helps guide the community through *dissatisfaction*, *exploration*, and into *sense-making*. He helps the community understand what it's experiencing. He is not the individual leader and singular change agent. He is coming alongside the community as they go through the process of change. He is not "leading the change" but helping the community create a new narrative within change. He helps them interpret what God is doing among the emerging realities, and he offers a new story, distinct, yet tethered to the historic legitimating narrative.

Jeremiah is no singular example of this process. Amos also offers us a portrait of a prophet called to the work of interpretive leadership. He shows us that God doesn't only use the appointed leaders and those who have the religious authority as professional ministers. In Amos 7:10-17, we see a standoff between a no-name prophet and the high priest, Amaziah. Amos—who has neither pedigree nor credentials, and does not stand on the platform of religious power—calls out Amaziah, who does have pedigree, credentials, and the support of the institution, along with the whole religious establishment.

Amos proposes a counternarrative that seeks to subvert the entire religious and political system. Amos teaches us that sometimes God uses small voices from small places, the tree-trimmers, and the ordinary heroes to topple empires. Whether you have official titles bestowed by the religious system or not, you may be the prophet called to the hard work of interpretive leadership in your own context. Mature prophets understand that this is a work of the body, not the acts of heroic solo leaders.

Jesus himself offers us the primary example of interpretive leadership by challenging the systems of his day. By the way, Jesus wasn't always "nice." He was quite adept at healthy conflict. The greatest prophet that ever was, Jesus confronted the dominant lifeworlds by reinterpreting scripture, in the sense that he quoted it often and claimed that his mission was to "fulfill" it (Matt 5:17). Yet his fulfillment, in some cases, is quite radical. This is made clear by his confrontations with the Pharisees and the "fulfillment" teachings: "you've heard it said . . . but I say" (Deut 24:1, Mark 10:2-9). In another example, Jesus changes the scriptural teachings of an "eye for an eye" *to* "turn the other cheek," and "hate your enemies" *to* "love your enemies and pray for them," and more (Matt 5:17-48).

Further, Jesus himself almost directly reframes sections in the book of Leviticus that speak of "clean versus unclean" sins requiring the death penalty, and the seemingly crude restrictions of those with birth defects, the deformed, or menstruating women not being allowed in community worship. This radical missional reading of scripture, his temple tantrum, and his unpopular position on the temple's inevitable destruction were profound disruptions to the religious system. It is obvious that this bold interpretive leadership was a deciding factor in his execution.

According to Mark, in Jesus's final teaching to his disciples, he instructs them to maintain a state of watchfulness and calls them to "stay awake" or "be awoke" (Mark 13:37). The instructions are not "wake up!" Here, the Greek word γρηγορέω (*grēgoreō*) denotes a process of continuing. We were awakened to the love of God embodied in the person of Jesus of Nazareth and available now by the power of the Holy Spirit. The church needs to recover from "amnesia" so that it can "stay awoke" again. Perhaps, just as the first disciples fell asleep in the garden, we as the church often fall asleep at the wheel.

Jeremiah (Re)Loaded Practices

Instructions: Create a space to discuss the relevant chapters of Jeremiah and to imagine what these practices might look like in your context. Consider making this a Bible study or a sermon series, and give people the opportunity to provide feedback.

1. Posture of permanence: build houses and live in them. In Jeremiah's context, this was about settling in to the new frontier. How do we find ways to do life with the people, neighborhoods, and networks where we dwell? What first-, second-, and third-places do we already have access to where we could start to gather?

2. Plant green spaces and eat. For Jeremiah, this was about settling in and utilizing the ecosystem. How do we create habitats of listening and encounter in the community where we live? How do we find ways to break bread with each other and people in our community? What potential third-places in our community could we explore gaining access?

3. Establish families among the people. In what ways has our congregation become exclusive? Does our congregation reflect our neighborhood? How do we enter the world of the other and embrace life in their tribes?

4. Seek the welfare of the other = the city where you are. We must ask the question, Who is our *other*, and how can we be *with* them? In what ways are we already blessing our community with no expectation of receiving in return? What are the ways we can love and serve our community? What connection points do we already have?

5. Disregard the dominant wishful thinking; it is deception. Jeremiah's greatest opponents came from within his own religious and political system. What lies are we telling ourselves that are "wishful" thinking and need to be confronted?

CHAPTER SEVEN

A Framework for Radical Innovation

After this the Lord appointed seventy others and sent them on ahead of him in pairs to every town and place where he himself intended to go. He said to them, "The harvest is plentiful, but the laborers are few; therefore ask the Lord of the harvest to send out laborers into his harvest. Go on your way. See, I am sending you out like lambs into the midst of wolves. Carry no purse, no bag, no sandals; and greet no one on the road. Whatever house you enter, first say, 'Peace to this house!' And if anyone is there who shares in peace, your peace will rest on that person; but if not, it will return to you. Remain in the same house, eating and drinking whatever they provide, for the laborer deserves to be paid. Do not move about from house to house. Whenever you enter a town and its people welcome you, eat what is set before you; cure the sick who are there, and say to them, 'The kingdom of God has come near to you.'"
—Luke 10:1-9

We strongly agree with Alan Roxburgh, and others, that Luke 10 is a key passage to missional engagement in our time. We see Luke 10 as a scriptural foundation for adaptive ecclesiology.

First, notice that the disciples are sent out two by two, in teams. All the disciples are sent, not just the twelve professionals. Their activity does reveal in some ways the future kingdom in the now as they seek to heal and bless communities in the power and name of Jesus. They assess the magnitude of the need and the lack of workers, and they start with prayer: "Ask the Lord of the harvest to send out laborers into his harvest." Then they become the answer to their own prayer as they go out into the harvest as laborers.

Notice the parallels with Jesus's missional blueprint and recent learnings from effectuation theory. There are no strategic steps toward some preconceived goal, no concept of constructing a building. The strategy is effectual, not causal.

Hence, go, acclimate yourself to the new communal scenario. Find a "person of peace" (Luke10:6). This resonates with entrepreneurs' ability to start with people they encounter in a relational sphere, rather than with a strategic process to find the "right people." This is an example of the "strategic partnership" principle.

Strategic Partnership: A key principle of effectual reasoning is to focus on building partnerships rather than concentrate on doing a systematic competitive analysis. Typically, entrepreneurs start the process without assuming the existence of a predetermined market for their idea; detailed competitive analyses do not seem to make any sense to them in the startup phase.[1]

Leave the baggage, travel light, "take no purse, no bag, no sandals" (Luke10:4). There is a clear parallel here to the "affordable loss" principle of the effectuation journey.

Affordable Loss: In contrast to causal strategy, where managers analyze the market and choose target segments with the highest potential return, entrepreneurs employ an effectual strategy. That is, they find ways to reach the market with a minimum expenditure of resources, such as time, effort, and money. In the extreme case, the affordable loss principle translates into the zero resources to market principle.[2]

Be comfortable with risk-taking, like "sheep in the midst of wolves" (Luke 10:3). Respond to emergent realities as they unfold, leverage contingencies, or go or stay based on how you're received (Luke 10:7-8). Your activity is shaping the future (the already and yet-to-be kingdom future, being shaped by present action) (Luke 10:9). There is a clear parallel here with the "leveraging contingencies" principle of effectuation theory.

Leveraging Contingencies: This principle of effectual reasoning is the heart of entrepreneurial expertise. It is the ability to turn the unexpected

---

1. Saras D. Sarasvathy, *What Makes Entrepreneurs Entrepreneurial?*, 3, https://dx.doi.org/.

2. Sarasvathy, *What Makes Entrepreneurs Entrepreneurial?*, 3.

into the profitable. Great entrepreneurial firms' structure, culture, core competence, and endurance are products of contingencies. In other words, the emergent systems are residuals of "particular human beings striving to forge and fulfil particular aspirations through interactions with the space, time and technologies they live in."[3]

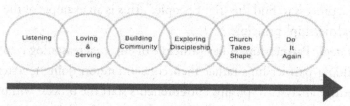

underpinned by prayer, on-going listening, and relationships with the wider church

Enter the work of your team. While there are variations, this is how a fresh expression typically develops:

Stage One: Listening

Many people pass right over this step and pay for it in the long haul. Partly because we are not very good at listening in the West. We are hard-wired by our culture not to listen. As Leonard Sweet says, "we live in an attention-deficit culture more adept at gaining attention than at paying attention, furiously beating the bushes that advance our interests while not paying attention to burning bushes that showcase God's activities."[4] There are burning bushes all around us, if we listen for the crackling.

The First Question: Who Is Our Other?

Listening is about asking the question, "Who is our other and how can we be with them?" In order "to heed the call of the other" we must in

---

3. Sarasvathy, *What Makes Entrepreneurs Entrepreneurial?*, 3.

4. Leonard I. Sweet, *Nudge: Awakening Each Other to the God Who's Already There* (Colorado Springs, CO: David C. Cook, 2010), 53.

a sense, dismantle the concerns of self.[5] We cannot have true rapport with out the kenotic self-emptying that Christ embodies in the incarnation (Phil 2). This is what Jesus calls "dying to self" (Matt 16:24).

If we believe that God is at core a relational being, that God desires to be in relationship with all humanity, and that, in our fragmented state, we have somehow alienated ourselves from God and each other, then our solution is to find ways to be with each *other*.

This creates a very different missional posture than we are accustomed to in the Western church. We have been deeply ingrained in a particular reading of the Great Commission in Mathew 28:18-20: "And Jesus came and said to them, 'All authority in heaven and on earth has been given to me. Go therefore and make disciples of all nations, baptizing them in the name of the Father and of the Son and of the Holy Spirit, and teaching them to obey everything that I have commanded you. And remember, I am with you always, to the end of the age.'"

The language of going out in the authority of Jesus to "make, baptize, teach, obey" has sometimes been used to collude with imperial power, to force-feed Western culture, rather than the Christian faith, to "all na-tions." The actual meaning of "go therefore" is better translated "as you go" or in the process of going, "along with" together.

Perhaps the posture of Jesus walking on the road to Emmaus is a more fitting approach: "While they were talking and discussing, Jesus himself came near and went with them, but their eyes were kept from recognizing him. And he said to them, 'What are you discussing with each other while you walk along?' They stood still, looking sad" (Luke 24:15-17; emphasis added).

Perhaps a *going with* is the missional model with the most potential on the new missional frontier. This looks like joining people in their daily walking, wanderings, and conversations, and listening them into speech and deeper understanding. Then, this also includes joining them at the table, where bread is broken and eyes are open to the presence of the risen Christ among us, when they urge us not to go away (Luke 24:30-31).

---

5.   Louise Nelstrop and Martyn Percy, *Evaluating Fresh Expressions: Explorations in Emerging Church: Responses to the Changing Face of Ecclesiology in the Church of England* (Norwich, UK: Canterbury, 2008), 94.

This is the Philippians 2, self-emptying, kenosis way of Jesus. This is the missional posture of Luke 10: "Carry no purse, no bag, no sandals." We come empty-handed, leaving the baggage of our preconceived notions behind. This often requires deconstructing long-held assumptions and encountering every person and community with a sense of wonder. We travel lightly, being sensitive to the Spirit's nudging as we go.

Who Is Our Sacagawea?

Identifying the "Person of Peace"

Being sent by Jesus is risky, sheep-among-wolves kind of stuff. There are unknowns. We are vulnerable. We travel lightly. We leave the baggage behind. Physically and emotionally, we come empty-handed and in a posture of listening. In our corporate business model of church, in which we measure success by institutional standards and risk by insurance policies, we have gone a long way from Jesus's design. Further, we don't come to fix, own, win, or take our community back, but to do life with the people we find there. To join our other in withness.

As followers of Jesus, we are not the trail-blazing pioneers; he is. There is nowhere we can ever go where Jesus, the "pioneer and perfecter of faith," has not already gone before us. All our pioneering is from a place of followership. On the new missional frontier, we need to lead with that distinction: we are always followers. Furthermore, we are dependent upon the "person of peace."

In Canoeing the Mountains, Tod Bolsinger retraced the footsteps of the explorers Lewis and Clark as an analogy for the kind of leadership we need in uncharted territory. Bolsinger comes to a profound truth when he begins to describe Sacagawea, the Native American woman who accompanied Lewis and Clark. Bolsinger says, "Sacagawea was not venturing into unexplored territory, she was going home."[6]

It wasn't some bold frontier to be conquered for this young nursing mother; it was the native land of her ancestors. During Lewis and Clark's expedition, she could connect them to the horses and resources

---

6. Tod E. Bolsinger, *Canoeing the Mountains: Christian Leadership in Uncharted Territory* (Downers Grove, IL: IVP, 2018), 191.

they needed, translate among the tribes, and navigate tense encounters. This woman led alongside the group, endured everything they endured, and had a voice in the decision-making. Bolsinger offers profound insight, which is applicable to adaptive ecclesiology across the missional landscape: "When you go off the map, the rules change."[7]

In Jesus's missional blueprint, we would call Sacagawea our *person of peace*. This is the person who calls our "uncharted territory" simply "home."

The call here is to do life at their table and eat what is set before us. We are the guest and not the host, and this is a profound change of posture for the Western church.

Featured prominently throughout scripture is the value of the table. The church started around the supper table, and Jesus's table practices are the foundation of the activity of the church today. He broke bread with sinners, tax collectors, sex-workers, and religious folks. Much of Jesus's activity was centered around the dinner table. Leonard Sweet has also strongly advocated for the church to "bring back the dinner table" as the center of Christian life and formation.[8]

Michael has started multiple "dinner churches" centered around this idea in his context. His congregations exist in the context of those experiencing poverty and food insecurity. These churches are built around the abundance of God's banquet table. As Graham Cray reminds us, "If there is to be no poverty in the new heavens and new earth, the church should be seen as a community that cares for the poor."[9] These dinner churches are a sign and foretaste of that coming reality. They are not just about giving away food to those in need, they are about building relationships.

Although prevalent, poverty is not always the only kind of fragmentation. Again, the most prevalent pain point in our postmodern scenario is isolation. While hyper-connected all the time through technology, the erosion of authentic community leaves us more alone than ever before. Fortunately,

---

7. Bolsinger, *Canoeing the Mountains*, 191.

8. Leonard I. Sweet, *From Tablet to Table: Where Community is Found and Identity is Formed* (Colorado Springs, CO: NavPress, 2014), 4.

9. Graham Cray, et al., *Fresh Expressions of Church and the Kingdom of God* (Norwich: Canterbury, 2012), 18.

the church can offer healing for this wound: communal life with Jesus. Even in affluent communities, God desires to heal the ache of isolation.

As we are in the process of double listening to our communities, we are seeking to form a community of withness through loving and serving.

Stage Two: Loving/Serving

In the Luke 10 missional blueprint, there is the following instruction: "whenever you enter a town and its people welcome you . . . cure the sick who are there." Cray reminds us that serving develops organically from our sincere to desire to listen. This serving is not manipulative or patronizing, nor is it oriented toward "fixing" the other. Rather, it "is an end in itself, a little anticipation of the new creation, whatever else may or may not follow."[10]

Healing often takes the form of loving and serving the people we find there.

This healing takes many forms. We think at one level, we need to expect supernatural healing when any form of disease may manifest. James 5 offers us a structure for how that can and should take place.

Then there are the gifts and skills that each of us brings to heal the other. Sometimes we bring healing to the other, through our life experiences and skills. Sometimes we bring healing through opening up channels to resources so that God can redistribute. Sometimes we bring healing through sitting in the waiting room, being present with a friend, as their loved one undergoes surgerye. Healing is never a one-way street; it is always a mutual exchange.

Stage Three: Building Community

In Luke 10, there is strong relational language of abiding: "Remain in the same house, eating and drinking whatever they provide . . . Do not move about from house to house . . . eat what is set before you." Cray says that "For many, belonging has to precede believing; acceptance by the

---

10. Cray, et al., *Fresh Expressions of Church and the Kingdom of God*, 21.

people of God must come before it is possible to understand and receive God's acceptance."[11]

Many times, we find that relationships are forming simultaneously with the exploration of faith.

Stage Four: Exploring Discipleship

Here, the community begins to grapple with Jesus's statement: "The kingdom of God has come near to you." This is where we begin to wrestle with what it means to live under the lordship of Jesus and become citizens of his kingdom.

Sometimes this is the most difficult transition to make within a fresh expression. Many are not satisfied with the language of "messy relationship" and "Spirit nudges." We are wired for causal thinking; we want steps and procedures that we can measure and replicate. Unfortunately, forming disciples of Jesus simply doesn't work that way. Each context is different, and there are multiple extraneous variables to consider for each person involved.

The good news is, we don't need to reinvent the wheel completely. We can lean into the wisdom of John Wesley and the early Methodist revival.

Wesley catalyzed a fresh expressions movement when he began to take it to the fields, the miners' camps, the debtors' prisons, street corners, and tombstones. While it doesn't earn him many fans in the inherited church, thousands of people began to respond to the Gospel and accept Jesus for the first time.

Wesley took new believers from a first encounter with Christ, through a life of sanctifying grace, to seeking perfection in love. He did this by connecting theological content to three major ministry structures: societies, classes, and bands. These different associations were an expression of the "way of salvation."

For each one of the waves of grace, there were corresponding formative elements to connect people to that grace. To represent prevenient grace, Wesley used the united societies. Any one could participate, Christian or not, who had "a desire to flee the wrath to come." Obviously, this language

---

11. Cray, et al., *Fresh Expressions of Church and the Kingdom of God*, 23.

needs to be updated. We don't want to scare people into the church, but the key idea is the inclusive nature of the society. Everyone was welcome. To promote justifying grace, he developed the class meeting. To advance sanctifying grace, he emphasized the band meeting.[12]

This reveals an immediate need for dedicated leaders. Overall, the early Methodist movement was sustained by the laity.[13] Under the leadership of the priesthood of believers, in a polycentric leadership model, a world-changing movement was released.

Fresh expressions is not about simply gathering in cool spaces to play church. Very real disciples are being formed in these very real microchurches.

For example, in Florida, the hundreds of fresh expressions being grafted into the inherited churches are harnessing the wisdom of Wesley's apostolic genius, creating structures that form people in the stages of grace using the model of societies, classes, and bands. Each of these fresh expressions is overseen by an adventurer, an "ordinary" Christian from among the "priesthood of all believers." These are usually not "professional clergy" people, but rather followers of Jesus who have been awakened to God's love and who have turned their passions into a church in the flows.

For instance, in Tattoo Parlor Church and Paws of Praise (church in a dog park), God's prevenient grace is at work, as they regularly engage non-Christians and so-called, "nones" and "dones," offering them Christ (a united society). In Burritos and Bibles (church in a Mexican restaurant), Shear Love at Soul Salon, and Yoga Therapy Church, God's justifying grace is at work as people open themselves to Christ, engage scripture, and feel free to pray publicly, take communion for the first time (for some), and share about "how goes it with their soul" (class). At Mascara Mondays

12. Steve Harper notes the genius, and often overlooked facet, of Wesley's methodology: he permitted membership in the united societies before conversion! Only a "desire to flee the wrath to come" was necessary. See Harper, *The Way to Heaven: The Gospel According to John Wesley* (Grand Rapids, MI: Zondervan, 2003), 122–23.

13. Alan Hirsch highlights Wesley's missional ethos and focus on discipleship as the reason for the movement's world-changing power. See Hirsch, *The Forgotten Ways: Reactivating the Missional Church* (Grand Rapids, MI: Zondervan, 2006), 103.

sanctifying grace is also at work, as a group of women gather in a coffee shop for the purposes of "single ladies learning to be sanctified and single" (band).

While these may not be perfect illustrations, you can see how they reflect a new/old Methodism that's remerging powerfully in 2023. While Fresh Expressions is a movement occurring across the Christian spectrum, we are convinced it may be one of the most Methodist things going on today. This is an old/new Methodism. This is a taking to the fields, "submitting to be more vile," "the world is my parish" kind of Methodism. This is about "making disciples of Jesus Christ for the transformation of the world." This is an awakening of Wesleyan people to our core missional narrative.

No matter what stream of the Christian faith you may belong to, these principles can be easily adapted to any context.

Stage Five: Church Taking Shape

Journeying with and among these mobile tribes in the daily networks centered on shared practices forces us to reconsider our inherited definitions of church. On this new missional frontier, the old strategies focused solely on people or locations are incapable of reaching the growing share of the population. This is church out in the blue oceans, the 60 percent that the inherited church will most likely never reach.

As we find ways to incarnate the Gospel in the space of flows, we need to engage people who form community around practices, in first-, second-, and third-places. Adventurers are like the border-stalkers who may or may not belong to the tribe but can move back and forth between the boundaries of the practice movements. These adventuring Christ-followers engage these practices through establishing an incarnational presence within the common community. Yet from within the community and its practices, the Spirit nudges the community toward the transformation of these practices, which "through shared actions and words, point[s] to the kingdom in such a way that the practice itself moves towards God."[14]

As we speak and enflesh the compassion of Jesus through listening, loving, serving, forming community, and exploring discipleship, the practices themselves are transformed. The expression begins to live under Christ's reign, which is reflected in the deep relational nature of the micro-community. The person of peace opens the gateway to authentic relationship, and Christ is powerfully present as the wound of isolation is healed. A contextual church is forming among the native practices as Christians and so-called "nones and dones" do life together. The Holy Spirit is transforming the dispositions of the participants as they enter more fully into the kingdom reign. Sanctification is occurring gradually, as the community moves through the waves of grace together.[15]

These fresh expressions emerge and take the shape and flavor of the people in these micro-communities and their practices. "Worship" takes many contextually specific forms. This does not mean fresh expressions are "worship lite." As Cray says, "The worship life of fresh expressions need not be minimal, it can be highly creative . . . Worship is transformative and essential to disciple-making. But it must be contextually authentic. Mature fresh expressions will also be eucharistic. A minority of fresh expressions begin with eucharistic worship, but all need to progress towards it, at an appropriate stage of their development as a Christian community."[16]

Tattoo Parlor Church did not start with Holy Communion. It took time for the community to progress into that stage. We did not show up at Burritos and Bibles with a chalice and consecrated tortilla the first night! Over time, the community intuitively and organically experienced a longing for more. Once we were ready, our servers at Moe's provided us a tortilla and some Hi-C from the soda machine. The contextual ingredients

---

14. Bryan K. Bolger, "Practice Movements in Global Information Culture: Looking back to McGavran and Finding a Way Forward," *Missiology* 35, no. 2 (2007): 181–93, 182.

15. Bolger, "Practice Movements in Global Information Culture," 182.

16. Cray, et al., *Fresh Expressions of Church and the Kingdom of God*, 23.

of the space became Holy Communion, and the staff, largely consisting of "nones and dones," joined us in the meal.

It may be the only place in the world where you can partake of the Lord's Supper with Jimi Hendrix, Lynyrd Skynyrd, Nirvana, Jay Z, or the Eagles playing in the background. This is not "worship lite." This is worship that resembles the most primitive form of the church: meeting in a public space, transforming culture and practices, and offering Christ in the flows of people's everyday lives.

We appreciate Robin Meyers's description of a "subversive 'colony of heaven,'" among the empires of the world.[17]

Stage Six: Do It Again

Fresh expressions are born pregnant. We multiply the whole people of God through releasing the "priesthood of all believers," and here lies the most powerful potential of the movement. In the blended ecology, lay people no longer find the highpoint of their existence is serving on a committee, reading liturgy, or leading a Bible study—as important as those things are. They are released in their gifts, passions, and practices as missionaries to the local community.

Every time a fresh expression has begun fully to form as a church, a team can look at planting another one. Most times, this will have already started to happen within the life of an existing fresh expression. There is typically already a conversation about who, where, and what the next one will be.

Stage Seven: Grafting

For inherited churches planting fresh expressions, there must be a seventh stage in the process: grafting. The wild branches must be grafted back into the inherited tree to create a new organism. This will primarily be the work of your "disruptive innovation" department. The fresh expressions

---

17. Robin R. Meyers, *Spiritual Defiance: Building a Beloved Community of Resistance* (New Haven, CT: Yale University Press, 2016), xvi.

are kind of onsite laboratories. As you send the "go" teams into the community, you release both a gathered and scattered mode of being.

In complexity thinking, grafting is about bringing together pieces that could lead in unexpected ways to a form of emergence: synergistic relationships occurring between inherited and emerging modes of church that result in a new complex system.

Under the broader umbrella of complexity theory, emergence refers to novel and coherent forms (structure, pattern, order) arising from the dynamic, synergistic, self-organizing interplay among elements at successive layers within a complex adaptive system.[18] It also refers to the irreducibility of the properties of the whole to the characteristics of its parts.[19]

The hope here is to create a form of symbiosis we referenced from Stuart Murray earlier: "The brightest hope for the church after Christendom is a symbiotic relationship between inherited and emerging churches."[20]

The focus of grafting is captured by the phrase symbiotic relationship. When local churches plant fresh expressions and live in the mixed economy for a period of time, tending the symbiotic relationship between the inherited and emerging modes of church, a new creation is birthed: the blended ecology. This symbiosis is a form of adaptation. Grafting is all about the tending of that relationship.

18. Omer Yezdani, , et al., "Theory of Emergence: Introducing a Model-centered Approach to Applied Social Science Research," *Prometheus* 33, no. 3 (2015): 305–322, 306.

19. Vladislav Valentinov, et al., "Emergence: A Systems Theory's Challenge to Ethics," *Systemic Practice & Action Research* 29, no. 6 (2016): 597–610, 597.

20. Vladislav Murray, *Church After Christendom* (Milton Keynes, UK: Paternoster, 2004), 122.

CHAPTER EIGHT

Discern

Call to me, and I will answer you and will tell you great and hidden things
that you have not known.
—Jeremiah 33:3

Adaptive Ecclesiology and the Tradition of Discernment

The adaptive church seeks to be both faithful and flexible. At the heart of this tension is relying upon a conscious spiritual practice that seeks to understand, know, and follow God's will. In the history of the church, this practice has been known as *discernment.*

Like diagnosis, discernment is a process that requires space and time. The following is a simplification and adaptation of work done by Chuck Olsen and Danny Morris.[1]

1. Framing and Reframing: Here we clarify the issue that is at hand, and we ask, "God, what is your will in this situation?" This is about arriving at a focus.

---

1. Charles M. Olsen and Danny E. Morris, *Discerning God's Will Together* (Nashville: Upper Room, 1997), 71–91.

2. Shedding and Purging: In the next step, we ask the question, "God, how can I let go of my preconceptions and prejudices?" This calls for humility in the leader.

3. Listening and Grounding: As we go deeper, we ask God for images, texts, data and stories relevant to the situation. This holds together a knowledge of the tradition and an openness to the Holy Spirit's movement.

4. Exploring and Weighing: Here, we are moving toward a decision. We ask, "God, what are the best options or paths as we move forward?"

5. Closing and Resting: We place our decision before God, saying "Here is my discernment." As we rest in this decision, we sense either a consolation or a desolation, a clearness or a confusion.

This process assumes the presence of God; it includes individual and corporate practices of seeking God's will (in this instance, those of the Jesuit and Quaker traditions), and it involves a posture of willingness to set aside our own will (some would describe this as our unconscious bias) to seek a higher and better way—God's purpose and providence.

All of us have had the experience of needing to make a difficult decision. At times the right path is not obvious, and at other times we may not trust our instincts or intuitions. The choice may not be between good and bad; it may be more nuanced, between two paths that have their own merits, neither better nor worse than the other. How do we make these kinds of decisions?

One of the resources that many Christians find helpful is the Jesuit practice of spiritual discernment. Jesuits are a religious order within the Catholic Church, and their lives are shaped by the Spiritual Exercises of Ignatius of Loyola. John Wesley was an enthusiastic reader of the Spiritual Exercises, and many of his writings and teachings reflect his familiarity with discernment practices..

The Jesuit model of discernment, which is five hundred years old, is very simple, and it is based upon asking fundamental questions:

- Does this decision lead me to a sense of peace, freedom, and consolation?

- Am I excited and energized?

- Does it seem that a door is opening?

- Does this decision create a sense of sadness, depression, and desolation?

- Am I despondent and discouraged?

- Does it seem that a door is closing?

The Holy Spirit, according to the Jesuit tradition, is always on the side of consolation. When God places a gift within us, there is rejoicing when that gift is discovered and released. This spiritual practice takes time for a sense or feeling to settle over a person. This feeling also comes when the individual claims the gift and moves forward, at least mentally, in the direction of that gift and away from others.

Discernment is the practice of seeking to make decisions that are consistent with God's will. Spiritual discernment is not relevant to actions that are moral or immoral. And spiritual discernment is always enhanced when our own internal testing of a decision is weighed alongside the wisdom and insight of a trusted spiritual friend. This is the value of corporate discernment.

Discernment of God's will is an essential practice for the adaptive church. In the practice of discernment, the church can navigate change—a cloud by day, a fire by night. When there is spiritual maturity, an adaptive ecclesiology joins a deep inner life, aware of the internal stirrings of the Holy Spirit, with a risk-taking outer journey into the lives of people in whom that same spirit is also mysteriously at work.

Our Role in Resurrection

If no one in the community sees the need for change, it is unlikely that resurrection can ever take place. It's like being in a state of denial when a loved one has died. Perhaps there is something to learn here from the story of Lazarus's death (John 11).

When Jesus gets to Bethany, he gathers with the people to mourn. In his dissatisfaction with the reality of sin, sickness, and death, he weeps. Then, from this place of withness, he offers an act of interpretive leadership; he confronts this scenario of death with prayerful and prophetic words of life (John 11:41-43).

Churches stuck in a loop where flourishing has ceased have often become comfortably unaware of the corpses in their community, the stinky stuff. They are caught in a bad metaphor. They are caught in a narrative of sickness and death. This leads to a powerful form of denial and the idealizing of the past—nostalgia. Resurrection begins with a bold, two-fold act of interpretive leadership. People from a position of being *with* must be the catalyst who will confront the amnesia state with a subversive act of remembering and calling forth to the future.

This is an act of releasing resurrection. It is a movement from darkness to light, from death to life. Only God can raise the dead, but God invites us to have a small role in the process. When Jesus showed up three days late and a dollar short to resurrect Lazarus from the dead, remember that he invited the people present to play a role.

He told them, "Roll the stone away." Immediately, people were uncomfortable with this request. They said, "Lord, you don't want to do that, there's some stinky stuff in there!" But when they do the physical act of moving the stone, the miraculous power of resurrection is revealed. Then Jesus instructs them to unwrap the still bound in burial cloth body of Lazarus. We have the power to move stones and unwarp burial clothing. Only Jesus has the power to raise the dead (John 11:38-44).

If congregations want to adapt, it's going to take people who are gutsy enough to roll away the stone and deal with the stinky stuff. Every congregation has some stinky stuff. Something is wrong; the body is sick, and whatever that sickness is has been hidden in a tomb and sealed with a stone. Something is binding the body, preventing it from growing, immobilizing it, restricting it from sentness. Exposing and dealing with that sickness is the messy stuff of adaptive leadership. Unwrapping dead stuff is not an easy task, which is why most leaders simply won't do it.

Not dealing with the stinky stuff allows a toxic loop to form. Thus, as Edwin Friedman describes organizations, so it is with the church: its reality becomes one in which "the most dependent members of any organization set the agendas and where adaption is constantly toward weakness rather than strength, thus leveraging the power to the recalcitrant, the passive-aggressive, and the most anxious members of an institution rather than toward the energetic, the visionary, the imaginative, and the motivated." This is the ecosystem of most declining congregations, and it takes courage to break that loop. Unfortunately, most leaders in declining contexts experience what Friedman calls "a failure of nerve."[2]

Find the Idol and Smash It

Leonard Sweet says, "Icons point to God, idols point to themselves." Throughout scripture, the most prevalent sin is idolatry. Over and over, the people continually break the first commandment: "I am the Lord your God, who brought you out of the land of Egypt, out of the house of slavery; you shall have no other gods before me. You shall not make for yourself an idol, whether in the form of anything that is in heaven above, or that is on the earth beneath, or that is in the water under the earth" (Ex 20:2-4). Breaking the first commandment leads us down the slippery slope of breaking all of them.

People are consistently fixated on the things that point to themselves, rather than on the things that point to God. We make idols out of people, places, and things every day when we place those things on the thrones of

---

2. Edwin H. Friedman, et al., *A Failure of Nerve: Leadership in the Age of the Quick Fix* (New York: Seabury, 2007), 12.

our hearts. A community that centers around idols cannot ever become a community that is an icon. We cannot point to God when we are busy worshiping things that point to us.

The prophets confront Israel for its idolatry with a multitude of images. They believed the captivity, exile, and destruction of the temple were all a result of idolatry.

All through the Exodus narrative, the people continually rebel against Moses's leadership. Thus, a journey that could have taken a couple months takes forty years. It is an excellent resource for a community involved in an adaptive challenge. It can literally be used as a playbook for some of the things that the community will face—people wanting to return to the "golden age" of slavery, grumbling over the manna from heaven and the quail from the sky, staging rebellions, purging, burning-out, frustrated leaders striking rocks—it's all in there! Every declining congregation has its "back to Egypt committee."

Perhaps the greatest lesson we can take from the wilderness wandering is how Moses deals with idolatry in Exodus 32. He goes up the mountain to talk to God, and he's running late getting back. So, the people take his delay as a sign that it's time to party. They attribute this whole incredible, supernatural exodus event as the work of Moses, "the man who brought us up out of the land of Egypt," rather than to God, an act of idolatry in itself.

A side note here: idolatry can be "pastor centered" in nature. When members of a congregation like their pastor, and when he or she does what they want (office hours, home visits, chaplaincy, fund raising, preaching "well," administrative oversight, or single-handedly evangelizing the community), they are happy and the church grows. Yet, a community centered on any person except Jesus is an idolatrous community. They're like Israel; if Moses is around, everything is fine.

However, because Moses was running late, Aaron formed a golden calf from the spoils of the exodus, and they got up early the next day and "offered burnt offerings and brought sacrifices of well-being; and the people sat down to eat and drink, and rose up to revel." Essentially, they worship a false god and then follow it up with an orgy.

This is sounding more and more like a real adaptive challenge. God catches wind of what is going on and decides it's time to destroy these crazy, idolatrous folks, whom God no longer sees as "my people" but now as Moses'a people. Moses reasons with God, primarily on the basis of, "What will the neighbors think?" when he says, "Why should the Egyptians say . . .?" God then has a change of mind, and Moses goes back down the mountain. But when he witnesses what's transpiring below, he breaks the tablets.

He finds a scene from "Israelites Gone Wild," then immediately takes the idol they made and "burned it with fire, ground it to powder, scattered it on the water, and made the Israelites drink it" (Ex 32:20). Before he does anything else, he deals with the idol itself, destroys it, and makes them consume it. Drinking gold will definitely cause a tummy ache, but notice the decisive nature of his leadership: he orchestrates the conflict. Before the purging, the violence, and the plague, he diagnoses the root problem: *the idol.*

Every congregation has idols over the course of its life. Something is not right. God is not on the throne. Something has become a golden calf. Once a team has done the diagnostic work, getting on the balcony, listening, learning, loving, and identifying the idol . . . smash it! Nothing creates dissatisfaction like idol smashing.

Interventionists and Triage Surgeons

Smashing idols will create a cascade of dissatisfaction and most likely some mutiny no matter how carefully we listen, learn, and love. John Kotter offers us a critical insight at this point; one of the major mistakes leaders make is allowing complacency to linger. To achieve change, a sense of urgency must be created.[3] There is a delicate tension in leaping to action, not getting on the balcony, and delaying the right intervention.

In The Villages, a community in Florida, Michael has often been called upon by desperate parents and grandparents to organize interventions for their children. Those calls began to increase when one of those interventions led to a miraculous healing from a hospice bed and became front-page news.[4] While doing pro bono interventions has become an ongoing part of his ministry, the intervention gift-set can serve many leaders well who face adaptive challenges.

In an adaptive challenge, someone, whether it's the "appointed" clergy person or not, will have to be a kind of interventionist or triage surgeon. In the 12 Step Recovery community, we have many powerful clichés. One of them is before we can ever get to step one, we have to get to step zero . . . "Step Zero: this stuff has to stop!" We'll use a nicer s-word than the common language, but step zero is about "finding a bottom that sufficiently horrifies you." Pain is a great motivator for change. It's about creating urgency, breaking out of denial, and realizing you need recovery to begin with. We describe this phenomenon by using the acronym G.O.D: Gift of Desperation. Many people and churches die before they ever get to step zero.

One of the declining congregations we served was completely convinced that it was the self-identified "friendliest church in town," even though its reputation in the community was one of being unfriendly, unwelcoming, and staunchly exclusive. There were significant levels of racism and ageism. However, it was so deeply embedded in its own narrative, the congregation was convinced everything was just fine. The fact that it hadn't had any baptisms of new believers in ten years wasn't on the community's radar. Attendance was holding at around sixty by attracting already-Christians in a tremendous population growth area on prime real estate.

---

3. John P. Kotter, *Leading Change* (Boston, MA: Harvard Business Review, 2012), 4.

4. http://www.villages-news.com/thankful-for-a-second-chance-man-embarks-on-daily-lazarus-walk/.

Essentially, the congregation added members at about the rate at which they died. Offering prophetic, interpretive leadership didn't go well. Our attempts to create urgency amounted to members requesting a new pastor. We decided to have an amicable divorce in one year. Perhaps Jesus is on to something in Luke 10:10-11: "But whenever you enter a town and they do not welcome you, go out into its streets and say, 'Even the dust of your town that clings to our feet, we wipe off in protest against you.'" If a congregation is locked deeply in a cycle of denial, we can expend a great deal of energy and effort to no effect. Not every church is willing to die in order to live. Every church we have seen God bring back to life had the "gift of desperation." Without dissatisfaction, we can never move into the rest of the change process.

Master Yoda says, "The greatest teacher, failure is." Every interventionist knows that interventions fail more times than they suceed. Statistics simply aren't enough because we largely underestimate the power of denial. People who have gone to jail multiple times, lost jobs, homes, family, and pretty much everything else will continue to use illegal substances while saying things like "I don't have a problem," or "I can quit whenever I want." Denial kills people every day, and it kills churches just as often.

To offer adaptive leadership we need to think like triage surgeons. As an itinerant clergy, one of the typical pieces of wisdom disseminated in our denomination like gospel-truth is, "Don't change anything for a year." From our experience, and the experiences of many other triage pastors, that is not always good advice. When you have done the work of deep listening and established a guiding coalition, you will need to change some things, or you may not have a year. Now, please understand, if you are sent to a church that is in good health, yes, that is a great rule of thumb.

If your church has been in significant decline for an extended period, more things will need to change than stay the same. The key is organizing people to catalyze meaningful, strategic change at the rate the people can stand it. Although most of the work up front is listening and establishing authentic relationships, it will have incredible value in the long run.

75

Let's be honest: churches decline and die because they are wounded and sick. We admire the integrity of doctors, who, as difficult as it may be, sit down and share the magnitude of a patient's situation. No one likes to hear, "You are terminal, and you only have months to live." We don't think many doctors enjoy telling their patients that news either. However, that is their job, and they must do it with unflinching honesty and compassion. It is sometimes necessary for adaptive leaders to do this as well.

Think about it. If you consult with your doctor and your body is riddled with cancer that needs immediate, potentially life-saving treatment, do you want your doctor to sit down and say, "Well, everything looks A-okay!" No, we don't. We want our doctor to be honest so we can design interventions that will potentially save our lives or start preparing loved ones for our coming death.

Adaptive leadership challenges are usually more complex than a single lifesaving surgical procedure. They require us to develop new habits and adapt to a new way of living. Are there healthy ways for us normal folks who don't like conflict to "orchestrate conflict" in healthy ways? To this question, we now turn.

CHAPTER NINE

Cultivate Habitats

*Then Jesus entered the temple and drove out all who were selling and buying
in the temple, and he overturned the tables of the money changers
and the seats of those who sold doves.*
—Matthew 21:12

At the simplest level, orchestrating conflict requires us to create environments where conversations can take place. Think of these habitats in the larger ecosystem of the church, containing *"holding environments", in the language of* Heifetz and Linsky. These are spaces formed by a network of relationships where people can gather to address difficult issues or wide value differences. This enables leaders to direct creative energy toward a conflict without passions exploding in a harmful way.[1]

We suggest three types of holding environments for adaptive ecclesiology.

Cultivating Habitats of Listening

First, we need to create *habitats of listening.* These are safe spaces where people can give voice to their fears, frustrations, and dreams. Many leaders make the fatal mistake of starting with talking rather than listening. We need to share the story of the Gospel, but we also need to listen to the people in our community. This includes studying the past of the

---

1.   Ronald A. Heifetz and Martin Linsky, *Leadership on the Line: Staying Alive Through the Dangers of Leading* (Boston, MA: Harvard Business School, 2002), 102.

congregations we serve, particularly the deep past. How did this church come to be? Who started it? What were the members like? What was the missional thrust of their actions? What sacrifices did they make?

Every congregation is like a Tel, with many layers of story sediment. Listening to understand is our spade to dig in.

Creating these habitats for the church historians, matriarchs, and patriarchs to share those stories is very important. We need to look past what congregations may describe as their "golden age" to get to the core narrative that birthed the congregation. If we want to awaken congregations from apostolic amnesia, we must dig until we find the apostolic impulse that birthed them. Phil Potter notices how many times throughout scripture God reminds the people of their history. This subversive remembering is especially prominent in the Old Testament. Potter found that "linking past, present and future is a powerful tool in opening people to the possibilities of pioneering a new future."[2]

A common mistake we make in a revitalization is not changing things too quickly, but rather changing things without honoring the past. There is a careful balancing act that needs to take place. Speaking of human cognition in general, the brain tunes out in contexts in which there is too much predictability; likewise too much change creates disorientation and people shut down.[3] This requires having sensitivity to the context. As we catalyze missional innovations in inherited congregations, we can maintain an umbilical cord to the deepest truth of the womb of the past. That nurturing womb is always a sending one.

A simple tool Michael often uses in consulting is called the "Remembering for the Future" timeline. In the innovation journey, this exercise is a tool to establish path dependency: the past of an organization directing its future possibilities.

This exercise always has a profound impact on teams. We simply gather the people and cover the entire wall of a room or fellowship hall with a

2. Phil Potter, *Pioneering a New Future: A Guide to Shaping Change and Changing the Shape of Church* (Abingdon, UK: Bible Reading Fellowship, 2015), 71.

3. Anthony K. Brandt and David Eagleman, *The Runaway Species: How Human Creativity Remakes the World* (New York: Catapult, 2017), 22.

roll of paper and give the congregation markers. We draw a timeline that goes back to the congregation's birth, mark a place on the timeline for "beginning" and "now," and then extend the timeline into the "future." We ask the congregations to date and describe significant moments along the timeline, give their perspective of today, and forecast into the future things they would like to see happen. This creates a habitat of listening, where people can celebrate the joys and voice the frustrations. It also pointed us toward mapping out a future.

Listening is also about pulling the data. While numbers and metrics rarely can capture the deeper spiritual realities of a local church (more on this later), they can be an effective tool to hear what the Spirit is saying to the church. Congregations tend to be optimistic about their current condition, often saying or thinking, "Especially if we would . . . just get back to doing this," or "so and so used to do that," or "When _____ was our preacher, this church was growing like crazy."

In the context of decline, the numbers can be used to give an honest reality check and create urgency. We also need to use questions to get at the realities behind the numbers. There are incredible demographic tools that can be used to understand the larger communal ecosystem: Natural Church Development, Mission Insight, and Peoplegroups.info, among many others. Use every tool at your disposal. However, nothing can supplement good old boots on the ground listening.

There are numerous creative ways to create pipelines of listening, including creating surveys, visiting people in their homes and workplaces, going on neighborhood prayer walks, creating ways for people to give feedback, and having regular gatherings where people can gather to speak and be heard.

Cultivating Habitats of Imagination

Leonard Sweet says, "If you want to change your life, you need to get a new metaphor." Metaphors carry us into new vistas of possibility. Metaphor opens us up the power of imagination. Imagination carries us forward into innovation. One of the saddest things about some churches is that they have lost the capacity to dream. In our apostolic amnesia, the imagination is sometimes the first thing to go. Hirsch tells us, "Change the metaphor, and you can change the imagination."[4]

Most churches are stuck in a bad metaphor that went stale long ago. Unfortunately, the institutional nature of the inherited mode stifles creativity and imagination. The church has mesmerized people into a false narrative—the Western imperial version of Christianity. While there are many positive aspects of the attractional model, through the professionalization of the clergy, it creates an unhealthy codependency with the congregation. We assume that only the highly educated, trained, and ordained leader of the group can inspire the rest of us. It inadvertently creates a mesmerizing effect centered on the positional leader of the organization.

Edwin Friedman speaks of "imaginative gridlock" which can occur not only in families and institutions but entire civilizations, who become "stuck in an orientation that confuses its own models with reality." Friedman argues that it takes adaptive leadership to catalyze a "fundamental reorientation" to break free.[5] The institutional nature of the Christendom way creates a culture of passivity. This breeds a docility and dull obedience among the congregation, ultimately putting a lid on imagination and innovation.[6] We will deal with how the Christendom mode nurtures a spiritual form of learned helplessness and suggest a process for breaking it later.

Sam Wells discusses how the key to redemption and to a flourishing life lies in the imagination: "We act in the world that we see, and we anticipate within the stories that have formed us; but we are often unaware of those stories, because we are surrounded by them as a fish is by the

4. Alan Hirsch and Dave Ferguson, *On the Verge: A Journey into the Apostolic Future of the Church* (Grand Rapids, MI: Zondervan, 2011), 105.

5. Edwin H. Friedman, *A Failure of Nerve* (Church Publishing, 2017), 33.

6. Hirsch and Ferguson, *On the Verge*, 54.

sea."[7] Exercises like Remembering for the Future, What is Church?, and others are ways to generate awareness of the stories and metaphors that are all around us but we never see.

Creating habitats of imagination is about giving people safe ways to deconstruct their assumptions and turn to wonder toward new possibilities. Worship should always be a habitat of imagination, where we present and re-present the story of Jesus in fresh, inspired, and challenging ways that unleash the force of the people's imagination. The counternarrative of scripture forces us to reimagine and reorganize our lives around new metaphors.

Cultivating habitats of imagination is about releasing the people to envision an alternative future. In our Western paradigm we often assume that a visionary leader will provide vision for the people. In the way of Moses, the heroic solo-leader goes up on the mountain, gets the vision, and brings it back to the people. Actually, vision is a work of the people, for the people, and emerging from the people listening together for God.

Churches need vision. However, they don't need verbose and overly specific vision statements. Perhaps what we really need is a mission metaphor? Afterall, the Bible offers us a kaleidoscope of images of what the church is like. Every local church can find itself in one of those scriptural images and make it their own, remixing it for their local context.

Vision is not about the eyes, it's about the ears. Discerning God's vision always begins with deep listening. One of the art pieces we use nationally in trainings, is a statue in Philadelphia called "The Preacher." It states in the inscription, "the preacher, he [or she] guided our ways". The figure's posture is one of leaning in to listen. The preacher holds his hands to his ears, as if to say, "Come on, tell me more." Most think of the posture of a preacher as one who is talking, but this statue illustrates that the preacher "guides our ways" by listening, he or she has a word to

---

7. Graham Cray, et al., *Fresh Expressions of Church and the Kingdom of God* (Norwich: Canterbury, 2012), 164.

speak. We listen to God; we listen to the people; then we can speak. The old cliché is true: "People don't care what you know, until they know you care."

We appreciate Andy Stanley's definition of vision as "a clear mental picture of what could be, fueled by the conviction that it should be."[8] We firmly believe a community will struggle to embrace a vision when it comes from outside. Vision doesn't emerge from the outside looking in, it comes from the inside looking out (Matt 6:22-23). Leaders can't super-impose "their vision" on the people but can only help the people discern God's vision from within.

Much of the work in our Habitats of Imagination is discerning God's vision. One simple way to continue to create regular church-wide Habitats of Imagination is monthly gatherings. At these meetings, which are often potluck, we can garner feedback and invite people to share their best recipes and the stirrings of their imaginations. Fresh expression testimonies can be shared, as well a celebration of successes and failures (failures get standing ovations at St. Marks UMC). Creating a culture where failure is accepted and expected is important for the blended ecology to work.

These habitats are places of fertile soil for wonder, where people can explore tentative hopes and articulate memories; they are a land of maybe, where the imagination is endlessly expanded.[9] For a people whose legitimating narrative is centered in resurrection, the ultimate disruptive act that turns the death-dealing cycles of business-as-usual upside down, our imaginations are truly unleashed beyond all boundaries. A church that can no longer imagine resurrection will never experience it.

A new vision statement will not solve an adaptive challenge. However, if we can boldly ask, "What if?" and catch a vision of what the Spirit is up to in our community, there is hope.

---

8. Andy Stanley, *Visioneering* (Sisters, OR: Multnomah, 2005), 18.

9. Cray, et al., *Fresh Expressions of Church and the Kingdom of God*, 165.

Cultivating Habitats of Conflict

It is a false assumption that healthy churches do not have conflict. Conflict is simply a tension between two people or two groups who disagree strongly on a topic or issue. Sara B. Savage and Eolene M. MacMillan demonstrate in their research that healthy conflict is good for traditional and fresh expressions of church. They name some of the factors that make conflict in the church difficult:

- the Norm of Niceness: good church people are supposed to be nice;

- anger and Forgiveness: good church people should not get angry and should forgive each other;

- co-dependency: you are never good enough;

- faith communities are complex;

- Attitudes towards whistle-blowers.[10]

Jesus was not always "nice" and was quite capable of healthy conflict. He spent quite a bit of time in conflict with the religious leaders of his day and, of course, there was the temple tantrum (Matt 21:12). A fake "niceness" breeds hypocrisy. If we are hurt, expressing our anger is a natural part of being human. Ever read the psalms? By trying to "help" people who are struggling, we can enable them never to grow, a toxic form of co-dependency.

Sharing in communal life with Jesus with a group of other sinners is a highly complex life choice. Not being honest about those complexities is unhealthy. When harm is being done in a community it should be called out and dealt with, not swept under the rug. We speak so much about speaking truth to power, but it takes more boldness to speak truth to each

---

10. Sara B. Savage and Eolene M. MacMillan, *The Human Face of Church: A Social Psychology and Pastoral Theology Resource for Pioneer and Traditional Ministry* (Norwich, UK: Canterbury, 2007), 57.

other in the church. Churches that seek out and embrace healthy conflict can thrive.

Thus, we must also create *holding environments* for conflict. As Phil Potter says: "Any change process, then, must begin with a brutal honesty about where we really are at the moment."[11] Brutal honesty usually gives birth to conflict. One fatal mistake we often make is to evade conflict rather than pursue it. Transformation cannot occur without it. There are great tools for handling conflict. We suggest *Calm: How to End Destructive Conflict in Your Church*, by Mary Gladstone-Highland, Christina Wichert, and Katy Stokes; also worthwhile are Patrick Lencioni's *The Five Dysfunctions of a Team, The Anatomy of Peace: Resolving the Heart of Conflict*, and *Leadership and Self-Deception: Getting Out of the Box*. Getting key leaders in a room and working through material like this can be hugely beneficial.[12]

Habitats of Conflict are sometimes most effective in an offsite scenario. Also, an outside facilitator can be useful at times. The key to this holding environment is creating structural, procedural, or virtual boundaries, where people sense enough security to address the real problems. The balancing act for the leader is maintaining an appropriate level of tension and keeping the stress at a productive level.[13]

In the churches we have served we regularly gathered teams to deal with conflict. Some of the folks on those teams have been some of the loudest oppositional voices to our leadership. A couple of them have even asked, "Why do you keep me on this team?" It is a mistake for a leader to surround him- or herself with only "yes people." We can sustain a heart of

---

11.   Potter, *Pioneering a New Future*, 25.

12.   Patrick Lencioni, *The Five Dysfunctions of a Team: A Leadership Fable* (San Francisco: Jossey-Bass, 2002); Lencioni, *The Anatomy of Peace: Resolving the Heart of Conflict* (San Francisco: Berrett-Koehler, 2008); Lencioni, *Leadership and Self-deception: Getting Out of the Box* (San Francisco: Berrett-Koehler, 2000).

13.   Ronald A Heifetz and Martin Linsky, *Leadership on the Line: Staying Alive through the Dangers of Leading* (Boston, MA: Harvard Business School, 2002), 102–103.

peace with people we don't agree with. It is far more productive to keep the opposition close.[14]

Furthermore, it is better to deal with opposition face-to-face in a Habitat of Conflict than to let it spread like a virus in parking lot meetings. Yes, there will be times people need to be asked to leave for the betterment of the church and their own souls. Ultimately, through patient and persistent love, some of our most vocal detractors made their own, healthy decision to leave the church, and some have become ardent supporters of the mission.

Creating a Habitat of Conflict offsite at a nearby retreat center, or another site away from the church property, can be very helpful. Teams have to learn how to work through the issues, hammer out a covenant, and establish boundaries around how we will treat each other. We always start these offsite gatherings with worshipping, having fun, and doing team-building exercises. Then we get down to the business of open, unflinching truth-telling and conflict. Now our team has very little restraint with articulating the problems and confronting each other on accountability and inattention to results.

Adaptive leaders need to know how to turn up or down the heat when it comes to orchestrating conflict. We will often be the target of people's frustrations with the process.

Earlier we noted Edwin Friedman's suggestion that we are called re-orient away from tasks and toward emotional processes. The actual relational work of loving one another through differences requires a healthy and self-differentiated leader.

The power of "presence"—the capacity to be an "I" while remaining connected to a "we"—requires us to be rooted in our core identity as God's beloved. When we are a safe person, people will sometimes vent to us or at us. In those moments we can center ourselves in our union with Jesus. We are not our work. Our soul is more than our role. We can be true

---

14.   Heifetz and Linsky, *Leadership on the Line*, 85.

to our own values and life vision while valuing and sustaining relationships with those around us.

When we are reactionary, or when we join the fray, we further fragment relationships. Only in the mode of "nonanxious presence" can we rightfully discern the emotional barriers and human factors beneath the presenting problems. Here we must resist the temptation to do the work for the people, but instead give back the adaptive challenge to the people. To this, we now turn.

CHAPTER TEN

Release People

Those who abide in me and I in them bear much fruit, because apart from me
you can do nothing.
—John 15: 1-6

The more I considered Christianity, the more I found that while it has established
a rule and order, the chief aim of that order was to give room
for good things to run wild.
—GK Chesterton

Finding a good heroic solo leader who can get the job done is not a viable strategy for adaptive ecclesiology. We suggest rethinking the very concept of leadership itself. In cultivating the blended ecology, we will borrow from complexity thinking. Leadership is an emergent phenomenon, which occurs in a series of relational interactions among agents; it's not simply a skill that one has but is an exchange of dynamic interactions within a complex system.[1]

This does not mean we don't need leadership, but rather that leadership is shared equally among members in the group. Leadership is a phenomenon of a complex adaptive system, where relationships are primarily defined by interactions among heterogeneous agents, rather than hierarchically.[2]

---

1. Benyamin B. Lichtenstein, et al., "Complexity Leadership Theory: An Interactive Perspective on Leading in Complex Adaptive Systems," *Emergence: Complexity & Organization* 8, no. 4 (2006): 2–12, https://georgefox.idm.oclc.org/login?url=http://search.ebscohost.com/login.aspx?direct=true&db=bth& AN=24083897&scope=site.

2. Lichtenstein, "Complexity Leadership Theory," 3.

A complexity view suggests a form of "shared leadership" distributed among teams. Thus, leadership does not lie in a single individual in a managerial role only, but rather in an interactive dynamic in which any particular person will fluctuate between being a leader and a follower. So, leaders enable conditions where a change process can occur, while not being the direct source of that change.[3] Organizational power is in fact purely relational.[4]

Diane Langberg, in *Redeeming Power*, explains how much of the harm and trauma within the church traces back to the misuse and abuse of power. When power is concentrated within only a few actors in the system, it actually diminishes the compassion and empathy responses. In systems where elevated social power is not shared equally, it leads to a diminished reciprocal emotional response to another's sufferings.[5]

Langberg reminds us that "Godly power is derivative; it comes from a source outside us. It is always used under God's authority and in likeness to [God's] character. It is always exercised in humility, in love to God. We use it first as [God's] servants and then, like [God], as servants to others."[6] Whereas institutional church systems seem to ground authority in position or gender and then require obedience to that authority. For Christians, "all authority is Christ's, and any derivative of that power given to us is to be submitted to him in love."[7]

However, these concepts are threatening to existing systems that want to consolidate and hold onto power. We see this manifested in the life of Jesus himself: "Because Jesus never wavered from choosing love and obedience to the Father as the driving force in his life, he was a threat to

---

3. Lichtenstein, "Complexity Leadership Theory," 3.

4. Margaret J. Wheatley, *Leadership and the New Science: Discovering Order in a Chaotic World* (San Francisco: Berrett-Koehler, 1999), 39.

5. Diane Langberg, *Redeeming Power: Understanding Power and Abuse in the Church* (Grand Rapids, MI: Brazos, 2020), 91.

6. Langberg, *Redeeming Power*, 22.

7. Langberg, *Redeeming Power*, 122.

both individuals and systems of his day, a holy dissident with a disruptive presence and disruptive words."[8]

While the form of shared leadership we suggest here is disruptive, it has deep roots in the very nature of the Holy Trinity. Father, Son, and Holy Spirit exist in a diverse singularity, not ruling over each other hierarchically, but in a continuous dance, making room for the other. The Trinity shows us how the body of Christ can function. This framework offers a solid foundation for the local church as a "priesthood of all believers," each of whom brings unique spiritual gifts to the body.

Michael Moynagh reminds us that organizations are sequences of conversations, in which any individual's contribution can catalyze change in the whole system.[9] Just as one word can change the flow of a conversation, one conversation can change the direction of an organization.

The community of leaders needs to create habitats where conversations can take place. Organizationally speaking, change occurs through a series of conversations.

An adaptive challenge is not about implementing strategic goals toward some preconceived outcome. It is not about an appointed leader, operating from a place of positional power, creating a new vision statement, and delegating responsibilities toward its fulfillment. That is the causation thinking of the corporate business world. If we do this action (cause), it will lead to this result (effect). In complex systems, like congregations, every action can have surprising and unintended consequences, both good and bad.

So, adaptation is very much about a community of leaders journeying through a series of conversations together. In this community of leaders, many kinds of leadership can emerge. Again, one that is essential is interpretive leadership. Someone has to awaken people to the fact that they are inhabiting a less-than-resilient ecosystem and show that an alternative path is possible. Earlier, we offered Jeremiah as a model for the kind of

---

8. Langberg, *Redeeming Power*, 110.

9. Michael Moynagh, *Church in Life: Emergence, Ecclesiology and Entrepreneurship* (London: SCM, 2017), 22–23.

interpretive leadership needed in the local church to release the Spirit's disruptive work of resurrection.

Interpretive Leadership: In the church, this is the work of shaping and resourcing a community of interpreters. Through deep listening to God, scripture, and context, this type of leadership can bring to the people's consciousness the reality of the legitimating narrative in which they live. Interpretive leaders also lead the community of interpreters in attending to the Spirit's presence and activities, which includes shaping environments around scripture in contextually sensitive ways and co-creating new social imaginaries.[10]

Imagine that, as the church, in our falling asleep at the wheel, we have careened into a ditch. We awaken together in our old church bus. As we get out to survey the scenario and assess the damage, we realize we have been asleep a long time. The highway has disappeared. Now flying cars are whizzing by at incredible speeds. The whole ecosystem has changed. The old roads we knew aren't even there.

We now need different types of leadership for this scenario. We need *relational, implemental, interpretive,* and *adaptive* leadership. We need relational leadership to hold everyone together under the stress of this nascent scenario. We need implemental leadership who knows how to repair the bus. We need interpretive leadership to say, "Hey didn't anyone notice things have changed? Even if we fix the bus, the road has changed. By the way, what is the destination now anyway?" We need adaptive leadership that can operate in the uncertainties, improvise, and find a way forward. Engaging the context, asking for directions, and collaborating . . . hitchhiking toward the future destination! We need a community of leaders, and each type of leadership, operating together.

Remember, adaptive leadership, concerns an innate ability to adapt to diverse, chaotic, and complex environments, thereby assisting

---

10. Mark Lau Branson, "Interpretive Leadership During Social Dislocation: Jeremiah and Social Imaginary," *Journal of Religious Leadership* 8, no. 1 (2009): 27–48, 29.

organizations and individuals in dealing with consequential changes in uncertain times, when no clear answers are forthcoming.[11]

Implemental Leadership: This concerns the implementation of a set of competencies and skills for experiments, systems, and practices by which we live out our identity and agency.

Relational Leadership: This concerns attention and activity patterns that discover, initiate, nurture, and sanction the human connections that comprise a social entity.[12]

Newsflash: no single individual possesses all the forms of leadership needed for adaptive change! Most likely, even a whole team is weak in some areas. This falling-asleep-at-the-wheel analogy is fitting, as it describes the language of journey, or the *movemental* nature of the church. If churches and denominations dig deep enough into our history, we will always find somewhere in our genesis—sentness.

Giving the work back to the people requires a courageous kind of releasing of people to flourish in their gifts, and to make mistakes while they do so.

Releasing refers to cultivating an ecosystem in which all believers, which form the priesthood, can live into their identity as apostles, prophets, evangelists, shepherds, and teachers. It is an intentionally movemental word. *Releasing* describes a process of allowing someone or something to move, act, or flow freely (or, perhaps more fittingly, to allow or enable to escape from confinement . . . to set free!). Like a slingshot, you apply tension and release.

Quite literally, the attractional only mode of Christendom has confined and incapacitated the full movement and maturity of the body of Christ. Perhaps not intentionally, but nevertheless actually. Like the allegory of Plato's Cave, many Christians have been chained to a wall looking at shadows, convinced that this manufactured reality is the only reality. Unaware of our imprisoned state in the cave, it's easier to stay confined

11. Alan Hirsch and Tim Catchim, *The Permanent Revolution: Apostolic Imagination and Practice for the 21st Century Church* (San Francisco: Jossey-Bass, 2012), 69.

12. Branson, "Interpretive leadership during social dislocation," 29.

and talk to the shadows than explore the potentialities of what could be. Adaptive ecclesiology allows us to emerge from the cave and explore whole new vistas of possibility.

For example, in our own denomination, our mission statement is to "make disciples of Jesus Christ for the transformation of the world." While there is a certain hubris in believing we can "make disciples" (for only the Spirit can do that), we can create graceful ecosystems and a system of apprenticeships that are conducive to the Spirit's disciple-making activities. The problem is we have largely not been "making disciples for the transformation of the world." Rather, we have been making good church members whose butts are for the warming of our pews in the Christendom mode. Even churches that are supposedly "lay driven" have unwittingly created a glass ceiling for so-called lay people. Perhaps one problem is in the omitting of the word Go in the great commission.

Disciples are not made sitting in caves staring at shadows. They are not even made by attending Bible study and worship for an hour each Sunday—no more than our teenage children become capable drivers by reading books and taking tests. They become capable drivers when we get in the passenger seat beside them and teach them how to drive in the process of driving. Jesus has entrusted the mission to the whole people of God. Under his direction and lordship, the steering wheel is in our hands. We need to equip the everyday people of God to drive us along on the journey.

Think about how Jesus formed his disciples. Disciples are made in the process of sentness. Jesus leads the community of disciples on a formative journey that resembles "on-the-job training." They learn in the process of doing, going, failing, using their gifts, and even succeeding from time to time. Perhaps a more fitting description than a "priesthood of all believers" would be an "apostlehood of all believers." We are a community of sent ones on a journey of sentness.

Consider the incremental innovation framework discussed earlier. The stages of dissatisfaction, exploration, sense-making, amplification, and being on the edge of chaos now release a bottom-up, self-organizing, new creation community. The community is in the process of becoming an adaptive culture. Releasing is about living into the transformation.

Moynagh reminds us that to ignore what he calls a "mega trend" of the Spirit's work in the world today would be a serious mistake. God is using individuals and local churches to reach out into the daily life of their communities through fresh expressions in a powerful way. Moynagh says it would also be a mistake to "play down how ordinary Christians can take the lead."[13] We refer to these Christians as "ordinary heroes" and adaptive ecclesiology requires "releasing" them to join the disruptive work of the Spirit in our age.

One of the most damaging realities of Christendom's assumed attractional mode is the professionalization of the clergy. We have created an artificial ecosystem, much like a Yellowstone without wolves, in which churches have a paid minister as the center of the community. This model feeds our consumerism culture, in that church attendees (consumers) come to a central location to receive what professional ministers (producers) provide.

As Dave Ferguson says, "I have little doubt that the biggest blockage to people-movement is the professionalization of the ministry of Jesus Christ." Dave goes on to say it creates two adverse effects: (1) the limitation of ministry to an "elite group," which ultimately replaces the priesthood of all believers; and (2) the diminishing and even eliminating of the God-given call of the people (the Laos) to be apprentices and agents of king Jesus in every sphere and domain.[14]

Beneath the levels of the bureaucratic sediment of Christendom, local churches lose their "why." The attractional model's focus on "putting butts in the pews" becomes the default why of the congregation. This artificial purpose inadvertently creates pew potatoes: Christians who ride the pine

---

13. Michael Moynagh, *Being Church, Doing Life: Creating Gospel Communities Where Life Happens* (Oxford, UK/Grand Rapids, MI: Monarch, 2014), 27.

14. Alan Hirsch and Dave Ferguson, *On the Verge: A Journey into the Apostolic Future of the Church* (Grand Rapids, MI: Zondervan, 2011), 293.

from the sidelines, but never have an opportunity to get into the field. People in these congregations have been unwittingly programmed into a state of learned helplessness, which refers to a strong feeling of helplessness accompanied by the belief that nothing one does matters.

The psychological phenomenon of learned helplessness has been a focus of research since the 1960s, when Seligman and Maier theorized that animals learned that outcomes were independent of their responses—that nothing they did mattered—and that this learning undermined trying to escape the stimuli. In a landmark study produced by Seligman and Maier in 2016, they indicate that their original theory "got it backwards." They now posit that passivity in response to shock is not learned, but is the default, "unlearned response to prolonged aversive events . . . which in turn inhibits escape." They propose that "passivity can be overcome by learning control."[15]

Thus, when we speak of learned helplessness in the state of inherited congregations, we mean in the sense of this groundbreaking revelation in neuroscience. This intuitive notion of helplessness, the belief that nothing one does matters, is not something that is "learned" but is an actual "default" of living organisms. The attractional church mode unwittingly enables people to exist in a spiritually passive default state. Ultimately, long-term congregants can become dependent on the church in much the same way one can become dependent on unhealthy relationships, substances, and instant gratification behaviors that ultimately short-circuit spiritual development and growth.

The Florida Conference of The United Methodist Church is failing-forward in this area, despite our many flaws and failures. By adopting the fresh expressions way and promoting it from the highest levels of hierarchal leadership, a massive wave of releasing ordinary heroes is taking place in Florida. Every year more fresh expressions are cropping up, many of them unique to their specific context. We are only planting the seeds of

15. Steven F. Maier and Martin E. P. Seligman, "Learned Helplessness at Fifty: Insights from Neuroscience," *Psychological Review* 123, no. 4 (2016): 349–67, 349, http://dx.doi.org/10.1037/rev0000033.

what's to come, but the goal of five hundred fresh expressions by 2025 is well under way.

Our focus is not really fresh expressions . . . it's people. If we identify, train, and release adventurers, there will soon be many more than five hundred fresh expressions. Adventurers come in all different shapes and sizes, and in every age and race. Most are laity and remain tethered to inherited congregations. Some are forward-thinking, innovative clergy. Each one of those fresh expressions has the capacity to become "church" in the fullest sense of the word, transform communities, and give life back to the existing congregations they are tethered too.

The good news is that all people can learn to overcome passivity and helplessness. Primary characteristics to catalyze this kind of learning include giving permission, experimenting, encouraging innovation, and celebrating failure. The blended ecology futurefits existing congregations, in such a way that an alternative path for spiritual expression is revealed. This opens the possibility for the doctrine of a priesthood of believers to become a structural reality within the local congregation. Each week, people are confronted with opportunities to lead from their passions and gifting and are encouraged to turn their everyday practices into church in the flows. People can be weaned from unhealthy dependency on the church, to become a microcosm *of the church*, which fosters spiritual development.

Every Christian takes his or her place among the body, and every church becomes a church-planting factory. The local congregation becomes a multi-site. Dave Ferguson rightly says that "If we are going to mobilize a movement, we have to unleash the power of God's people."[16]

We want to suggest that the five APEST types (apostles, prophets, evangelists, shepherds, teachers) are five "keystone species" in every local congregation. Local churches need to cultivate "habitats," from which these five species can be released. This will potentially result in a form of emergence that will transform communal ecosystems and revitalize

16. Hirsch and Ferguson, *On the Verge*, 293.

existing congregations. Now, let's return to the phenomenon of trophic cascades.

The reintroduction of wolves into Yellowstone National Park released a trophic cascade that transformed the ecosystem at a fundamental level. Similarly, a remixed ecosystem emerges at the local church level, as we "release the wolves" that create trophic cascades transforming the ecosystems themselves.[17] The "wolves," or the "keystone species," are the apostles, prophets, evangelists, shepherds, and teachers in your community, and they are in every community. We just have to look for them. Trophic cascades teach us never to underestimate the power of small, incremental change.

Keystone species, from an evolutionary biology perspective, refers to species whose behavior impacts multiple other species in an ecosystem. The removal or addition of this species can change the ecosystem drastically.[18] In the church sphere, all Christians are keystone species in the way of five-fold apostles, prophets, evangelists, shepherds, and teachers.

Most declining congregations are in an artificial ecosystem scenario. Some of the essential keystone species are missing or have been domesticated into a state of learned helplessness. To experience the remixing power of resurrection, they need to be released again.

The initial training is minimal; it's simply about discovering and releasing. We have embraced the Fresh Expressions UK model of low initial training, high ongoing support.[19] However, these small adjustments have big potential.

Most declining congregations that resemble the Yellowstone scenario have embraced the collapsed narrative of Christendom, which has created

---

17. J. A. Estes, and John Terborgh, *Trophic Cascades: Predators, Prey, and the Changing Dynamics of Nature* (Washington DC: Island, 2010). Also, watch "How Wolves Change Rivers" on YouTube at https://youtu.be/ysa5OBhXz-Q.

18. Seth B. Magle and Lisa M. Angeloni, "Effects of Urbanization on the Behaviour of a Keystone Species," *Behaviour* 148, no. 1 (2011): 31–54, 33, doi:10.1163/000579510X545810.

19. Louise Nelstrop and Martyn Percy, *Evaluating Fresh Expressions: Explorations in Emerging Church: Responses to the Changing Face of Ecclesiology in the Church of England* (Norwich, UK: Canterbury, 2008), 48.

an artificial ecosystem. The people exist in the default mode of helplessness. To create a new ecosystem, we will need to release the wolves. Initially, a "no wolves" scenario seemed like a good idea at Yellowstone; it protected the vulnerable, less predatory animals like deer. However, an ecosystem without wolves is an artificial scenario. As seemingly violent and predatory as wolves are, they are necessary life forms for the health of an ecosystem. Yes, wolves kill deer sometimes, but they also give life in many other ways. As a keystone species, they shape the behavior of all others in the ecosystem.

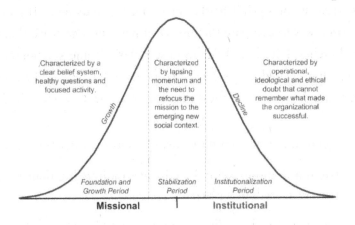

Some scholars describe the decline cycle as the "institutional" period, although we find that language unhelpful. As J. R. Woodward reminds us, institutions themselves are not a bad thing; institutionalism is a bad thing.[20] We need to sustain the good parts of our institutional identity while recovering our movemental identity as well. In the blended ecology the two work together.

Regardless, when congregational systems begin to experience decline, they will also place incredibly unrealistic expectations on their clergy. The expectation in this typical McDonaldized Christendom scenario is that

---

20.   J. R. Woodward, *Creating a Missional Culture: Equipping the Church for the Sake of the World* (Downers Grove, IL: IVP, 2012), 41.

we hire the paid professional minister to take care of our needs. The professional pastor is the producer of religious goods and services, while the congregants are the consumers. This is an ideal scenario in a Christendom context, where many people identify as Christians and feel they have a moral obligation to the "state religion." They will find a church nearby and join the one that most fulfills their consumeristic needs (entertaining music, provocative preaching, youth and children's programs, etc.).

This is a death-dealing scenario this is not sustainable at many levels. Research by Dave Olson—director of American Church Research Project, which gathered data from two hundred thousand churches in the United States—reveals the up-hill battle older congregations face. The focus of his research was to compare the impact of new churches with that of existing churches. Hirsch and Ferguson summarize some key points of the data, which measured the percent of yearly growth based on the decade in which a church was started; the data collected spanned two hundred years:

- eighteen out of twenty-two decades show negative growth;

- two out of those twenty-two decades indicate less than 1 percent growth or a plateau;

- only two decades indicate a positive growth rate, and the first positive indicator is among churches started in the last ten to twenty years (a little more than 2 percent growth rate);

- however, new churches started in the last ten years grew on average by 9 percent.

Here's the key importance of this data: "New churches have three to four times as many conversions as do established churches . . . in the first ten years, new churches grow twenty-three times as faster than churches over ten years old."[21]

---

21. Hirsch and Ferguson, *On the Verge*, 252–53.

Once our older congregations cross a certain line of sustainability into decline, the probability of revitalization is very low, as illustrated by the Sigmoid Curve, below.

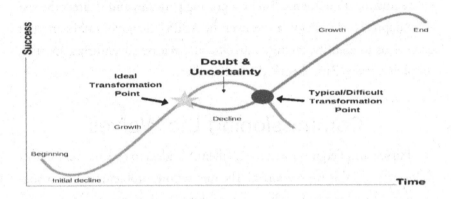

To experience revitalization, older churches are going to have to start planting new churches to reverse this trend in the form of this "S curve." This is the power of the blended ecology way; it allows churches with significant history in communities to become multi-site. While the fresh expressions may not resemble the inherited form, it allows churches to reach people in the community the traditional church cannot. The key to success here is not expecting more from already exhausted clergy but releasing the people of God. We have seen adopting the fresh expressions approach and restructuring in the blended ecology way revitalize congregations beyond even the difficult transformation point.

The Christendom mode alone is no longer a viable approach for the North American church. Many pastors are trained and educated to fulfill the role of professional minister. Pastoral ministry has one of the highest burn-out rates in all vocational fields. An overwhelming majority of all new clergy will not be in ministry after five years of service. They are often capable, loving, gifted pastors who serve their people well. Unwittingly, they take on the role of personal butler to a version of Christianity that is not sustainable.

Clergy in this new missional frontier are called to be wolves. While they don't need to eat anyone (!), they will have to disrupt the toxic cycle, create missional mess, establish new grazing patterns, and redirect the rivers. Adaptive ecclesiology can recover the APEST design of Ephesians 4. It enables us to identify, recruit, cultivate, and release adventuring apostles, prophets, evangelists, shepherds, and teachers.

Commissioning the Wolves

Hirsch and Ferguson write, "Challenge leaders to ordain every Christ follower."[22] To this we say, amen! The one serious problem with that suggestion is that for some, technically speaking, within our own system, we might have no authority to do that. The good news is, we don't have to. We believe a kind of ordination takes place in the baptism of every believer. We are ordained not by receiving official credentials from an institution, but by the power of the Holy Spirit that claims us in the grace-filled waters of our baptism and gives us a new identity and a greater purpose. In our baptisms we are ordained into the priesthood of believers.

As beautiful and profoundly true as this is, it is still imperative that we have some formal biblical process to acknowledge and release the wolves into the ecosystem. This will require the local congregation regularly to commission these apostles, prophets, evangelists, pastors, and teachers to their local communities. We can operate with integrity in the specific polity of our denomination while finding ways to recover the apostolic scriptural practice of preparing and commissioning through the laying on of hands—local missionaries.

In our congregations, laity teach, preach, counsel, pray, offer care, and plant churches through the community. Our *United Methodist Book of Worship* has special services for the commissioning of these people in

---

22. Hirsch and Ferguson, *On the Verge*, 266.

leadership. This is a remnant of our roots as a missional renewal movement largely sustained by laity.

However, the blended ecology requires us to remix our inherited leadership structures at the local level. This requires adaptation and courage.

CHAPTER ELEVEN

Fail

He has told you, O mortal, what is good,
and what does the Lord require of you
but to do justice and to love kindness
and to walk humbly with your God?
—Micah 6:8

The Adaptive Change That God Desires

At its worst, to avoid complex conversations about racial dignity or sexual identity, especially as these are rooted in the image of God in each person, and to avoid this by saying "let's make disciples," is to focus on a technical rather than an adaptive challenge.

To be a disciple of Jesus, a student of his teaching, is to learn from the way he did not avoid complex questions about identity or boundaries. This would become increasingly true in the book of Acts, as his disciples would seek to be his witnesses in Jerusalem, Judea, Samaria, and to the ends of the earth (Acts 1:8).

Jesus, in his discipling was profoundly adaptive by nature—you have heard it said, but I say to you. Jesus, in his person, was profoundly adaptive—the word was with God, and the word was God . . . and the word become flesh.

The mission of God is adaptive, or we might even say that God's nature is adaptive for the sake of the mission. Though he was in the form of God he emptied himself. Kenosis is adaptation.

This is the transformation to which a follower of Jesus undergoes. To become more Christ-like, to become more godly, is to experience the renewal of our minds and the circumcision of our hearts.

If we are honest, we avoid complex conversations like these because they represent a kind of death. As the Apostle Paul wrote: "I have been crucified with Christ, and it is no longer I who live, but Christ who lives in me. And the life I live in the flesh I live by faith in the Son of God who loved me and gave himself for me."

The adaptive change that God desires is precisely the adaptive change that God has already undertaken for us, and for our salvation.

At Times, We Have Preferred Technical Change

"The most common cause of failure of leadership is produced by treating adaptive challenges as if they were technical problems."[1]

The church that represents Jesus genuinely wants to be fruitful, effective, and transforming. And yet, at times, we have gone about this in technical ways. In one season we noticed an absence of families, in a way that seemed different from a previous generation. These had often been homogeneous families, often representing one ethnicity, with perhaps several children. This began to change.

And so, well-intentioned leaders in churches across the United States responded in technical ways. We build pre-schools for children, gymnasiums for youth, and, at times, private schools for the entire educational span, from early childhood to late adolescence.

---

1. Ronald A. Heifetz and Marty Linsky, *Leadership on the Line: Staying Alive through the Dangers of Leading* (Boston: Harvard Business Review Press, 2002), 19.

We thought, "If we begin a school, if we build a gym, the children will come, the youth will come, the parents will come." And, in our unspoken thoughts, we will recapture the church of a former time.

Nostalgia. But nostalgia is not adaptation.

These strategies, and they occurred in the best of churches and among the best of leaders, were based on assumptions like "Others will change their behaviors and join us" and "The attraction model will work for us."

And yet, we were unable either to attract or retain younger generations. Some of the reasons are cultural, some theological and ecclesiological.

As the Fresh Expressions movement taught us, the parish-based system was dying. Biology was not destiny. As the spiritual classic framed it, "disciples are made, not born." We had assumed that if they were born Catholics, they would remain Catholics, or return to Catholicism when they had their own children. Substitute Methodist or Evangelical or Episcopalian.

The technical solutions we sought to help facilitate these outcomes did not achieve these results.

To become a disciple is an adaptive change. To be a church that makes disciples is adaptive ecclesiology.

We needed to do a deeper diagnosis. We needed to get on the balcony and see the broader patterns of God's way of working the in the world. The church was not central to life in ways it had been post-World War II, in what Gil Rendle called an aberrant time. And the family was changing (more about that later). Yet, God is very much alive. Praise God! Jesus is risen and the Holy Spirit is present with power.

To diagnose, to gain a balcony perspective, is to live again in a holy space—the gospels call it the "upper room." It is to pray, to wait, to trust. Adaptive change is mystery, messiness. The technical has its place. But an adaptive ecclesiology is the way to renewal.

Metrics

One of the ways we engage in technical rather than adaptive leadership is in the way we use metrics:

- our average worship attendance;

- our average Sunday School attendance;

- our average weekly financial giving.

Metrics are important, and they measure a part of what is going on. Our use of metrics can also convey or hide our bias. Some questions to ask are:

- Do we measure in person worship attendance but not online participation?

- Do we measure attendance in a sanctuary but not in a Fresh Expression?

- Do we measure the time people give to service, or the number of people serving in mission?

There is a profound adaption occurring in our local churches. People may care deeply about a ministry that a church barely measures. And, indeed, in failing to measure we may be communicating that the ministry does not really "count"!

Such a ministry could be:

- a daily practice of contemplative or centering prayer;

- a weekly gathering of those struggling to overcome addiction;

- a monthly respite for parents of children with a disability;

- a yearly gathering to advocate for the rights and living conditions of the imprisoned.

Our metrics must become adaptive. Adaptive metrics will help us to gain a narrative of who we really are as a church. These are essential to an adaptive ecclesiology, but they are not the whole story.

More Than Metrics

Another way we lapse into technical rather than adaptive thinking is by treating people as numbers rather than narratives.

Narratives are messy, mysterious, and . . . adaptive. A man's wife suffers from dementia. They are unable to worship on a regular basis in the church's sanctuary. Their journey together may indeed be one of profound meaning, mystery, love, and loss.

There is really no technical fix for this couple. The adaptive church responds faithfully by extending friendship and surrounding them in prayer. An online service adapts to their life situation, as an orderly sanctuary cannot.

Theirs is a narrative that cannot be measured or even described in technical ways. The adaptive church recognizes a person, a couple, a larger community, even an epidemic of people, suffering from this disease. The estimate of people with dementia by the Institute for Health Metrics and Evaluation is 153 million by the year 2050; that is triple the present number.[2]

What does this mean for an adaptive church?

And how might the adaptive church "see" other people groups? Consider the following:

- people on the journey through or beyond divorce;

- people returning home from incarceration;

- single parents;

- parents of LGBTQIA+ children;

- undocumented immigrants.

---

2. See the profound work of Kenneth L. Carder, *Ministry with the Forgotten: Dementia Through a Spiritual Lens* (Nashville: Abingdon, 2019).

Which groups does your church struggle to see? How would you add to this list?

Failing Forward

To unleash the local church as God's mission force to create trophic cascades that will transform ecosystems, we need to recover *a theology of failure.*

Embracing the newest season of our lives as grandpas, Michael and I have been spending as much time as possible with grands. They teach us a lot. Have you ever watched a toddler learn shapes through playing with a shape cube? It's an amazing trial-and-error process through which the pre-schooler learns shapes. During this failing-forward experience, the toddler bangs the shape box with the different shapes. As a consequence of trying to force the square into the circle, the hexagon into the rectangle, and the star into the oval, the child learns the proper shapes to fill those spaces.

We liken the process of following Jesus to this failing-forward kind of learning, and it has certainly been our experience in the Fresh Expressions movement. When we read the scriptures, we are comforted to find that Christians have always failed forward. Our friend Peter probably offers the clearest examples:

- walking across a tempest-tossed sea, until, of course, he almost drowned himself (Matt 14:28-30);

- trying to cast demons out of Jesus (Matt 16:22);

- cutting people's ears off with a sword (John 18:10);

- denying that he even knew Jesus (Mark 14:66-72).

Albeit, at least Peter did the things the other disciples were too faint-hearted to attempt. Nevertheless, it seems Peter was kind of an expert at failure. Of course, he was in good company, with tricksters like Jacob, murdering fugitives like Moses, adulterers like David, and terrorists like

Paul. Oh yes, the great cloud of witnesses who failed forward epically, yet whom God used in incredible ways. And a great cloud of "forward failers" marches on!

Even so-called 'failed' fresh expressions lead to heavenly celebrations when one lost one comes home. So, we just keep failing forward like a focused toddler banging on a shape cube—crying when we miss the mark, break something, or watch a lost one head back to his or her old life. We giggle wildly when we get a square in the right hole. We laugh out loud when all the pieces fit, and hugging and applauding each other when they don't.

Most of the time we are playing as we learn, quite convinced that following Jesus is fun the majority of the time. Whether we get it right or wrong, we learn, and we find the great cloud of witnesses who have gone failing forward before us cheering us on (see Heb 12:1).

Here's a helpful cliché: "Follow to lead and get out of the way." In releasing the keystone species to transform ecosystems, leadership is mostly about following Jesus, then getting out of the way. As we are drawn into the life of the Trinity, caught up in the circle dance of perichoresis, we travel through the first-, second-, and third-places connected by flows of a network society. We offer withness and communal life with Jesus. We release the innovators into the larger communal ecosystem to fail forward on a journey of missional mess-making.

The Art of Mess-Making

Releasing the wolves in Yellowstone initially created some mess. Adaptation is not a sanitized process. Confronting the toxic stinky stuff that has been hidden away in the tomb is not for the faint of heart. Disruption, by its very nature, creates a mess.

Alan Roxburgh describes how leaders will need to use disruption to create just enough mess to shake up the local church, without causing a complete system breakdown. He refers to this as an "art" that involves listening well to the Spirit and to the congregation.[3] This is our "edge of chaos" in the process of ecclesial innovation.

Formation of the early church in the book of Acts is anything but neat and clean. At the very best, the disruptive work of the Spirit, coupled with the improvisational responses of the disciples, were responses to the messy emerging missional needs. In Acts 15, we get the sense that Antioch was becoming disruptive to the church in Jerusalem. Leaders are sent to investigate, and they are troubled by the emerging mode of church there. It seems this Gentile version of Christianity was running wild in disruptive ways. The Antioch leaders were not requiring Gentile converts to be circumcised or obey the fullness of the law.

This creates dissatisfaction and sends the early church on a journey of exploration, sense-making, and amplification. There, on the edge of chaos, this incredible challenge shapes the future of the church. How the early church handled this disruption changed the course of world history. Amid the mess, they came together and made some serious concessions so that the church would continue to grow and thrive among the Gentiles. What they were doing is called Spirit-led, prayerful, scripturally-grounded . . . *improvisation.*

Improvisation is the process of devising a solution to a problem by making-do, despite the absence of resources that might be expected to produce a solution. In a technical context, this can mean adapting a device for some use other than that which it was designed for or building a device from unusual components in an ad-hoc fashion.

In the context of decline, resurrection is a disruption of the death cycle. That doesn't happen by being a people pleaser. It won't be an easy process. There will be mutiny and resistance. However, if this doesn't happen, it's unlikely the process of resurrection will be released.

Bolsinger reminds us that in changing the DNA of living organisms through birthing something new—the child of that new birthing won't be

---

3. Alan J. Roxburgh, *Missional: Joining God in the Neighborhood* (Grand Rapids, MI: Baker, 2011), 174.

all one party or the other but a new living culture that combines the past and the future. Bolsinger goes on to say that you must really communicate love to the other party, or that other party will not let you get close enough for an exchange to take place that can lead to a birth.[4] Thus, transformation through giving birth starts with getting lucky! This is an accurate description of the interaction that takes place in the blended ecology way. As you care for the existing congregation and start new experiments in the community, a new creation is born. In symbiosis, tending the relationship is essential.

Harford also touches on how disorder can lead to improvisation, and how masterpieces can emerge from the mess. When we engage the disruptive work of futurefitting congregations, it releases a nascent chaordic form. The kind of leadership that is needed is not so much organizational, but improvisational. Again, think effectual rather than causal. Perhaps the Jerusalem and Antioch gathering is a microcosm of every local congregation that attempts to restructure in the blended ecology way.

Mess-making is an art that is largely dependent on improvisation, intuition, and innovation. There are no formulas to do it properly. It requires the kind of Spirit-led listening that Roxburgh describes. The phenomenon of trophic cascades helps us better understand this process.

The ultimate goal of the kind of adaptation the Lord requires is this: "He has told you, O mortal, what is good, and what does the Lord require of you but to do justice and to love kindness and to walk humbly with your God?" (Micah 6:8). The compassion of Jesus, embodied in healing ways, is the core motivation for adaptive ecclesiology. And this requires courage.

---

4. Tod Bolsinger, *Canoeing the Mountains: Christian Leadership in Uncharted Territory* (Downers Grove, IL: IVP, 2018), 82.

See the Systems

Abide in me as I abide in you. Just as the branch cannot bear fruit by itself unless it abides in the vine, neither can you unless you abide in me. I am the vine, you are the branches. Those who abide in me and I in them bear much fruit, because apart from me you can do nothing.
—*John 15:4-5*

I think continually about what Christ meant by the afterlife, and for me, it's that when you are disavowed of the illusion that the material will fulfill you, you enter the Kingdom of Heaven. The Kingdom of Heaven is spread upon the Earth.
—*Russell Brand*

We all inhabit complex networks, living systems. A diversity of relational habitats is interconnected and affecting the larger ecosystem. In the initial stages of leading incremental progress, the "Three L's", listen, learn, and love, are essential.

Listening: This is about listening to understand *not* to respond. In fresh expressions we speak frequently of "double listening" to God and the context. Listening to God is about prayer. We need to spend time in conversation with God, but mostly listening to what God is saying.

To lead a congregation through an adaptive process we need to cultivate an intentional communal prayer life. In many cases people have stopped really praying, except in the sense of a routine of prayer to fulfill their religious responsibility. Some practices to invite people to more intentional prayer, can be a Luke 10:2 prayer initiative, in which the congregation pauses at 10:02 each day to pray the missional prayer of Jesus, to notice the harvest, to ask for workers, and to become the answer to our own prayers. Also, prayer walking, praying for strangers, attending weekly prayer gatherings, and offering a pray for the pews campaign could be helpful.

Listening to the congregation is simply about finding ways to hear people's stories, hearing how God is speaking through their lives, and listening to people's struggles and the hopes. It is listening to the sounds that are breaking God's heart there.

Learning: This is about discovering who these people are. What is the language they speak, what is their theology, their history? How do they deal with conflict? What are their dreams? What are their values? It's about assuming a posture of *kenosis*. It's self-emptying. And this requires self-awareness. It's coming into relationship with each other, not to fix, own, or manage, but to understand. It's more about asking questions than giving answers. It's about a desire to bless.

Loving: This is about becoming other-oriented. It's an intentional effort to care for people, even if they may not care for you. It's about hearing the hearts and the needs of the people in the community.

The three L's are really about *withness*. We appreciate Leonard Sweet's definition of withness in the sense of, "indispensable relationships." He reminds us that before followers of Jesus can ever be a witness for Jesus, they must first be a withness.[1] We are not much of a witness to Christ if we don't have an indispensable relationship with him. This profound truth can easily be applied to the relationship between a clergy person and a congregation. Withness comes before witness.

When a people know you are truly with them, it creates a relational dynamic that cultivates trust. People will typically go with you into uncharted territories when they know you are with them. No matter how small or large the congregation may be, we need to find strategic ways to

---

1. Leonard I. Sweet, *11 Indispensable Relationships You Can't Be Without* (Colorado Springs, CO: David C. Cook, 2008), 20.

be with people, to listen, learn, and love. At the same time, we need to find ways to be with the people in the larger community as well.

When Michael arrived at Wildwood, he took the office door off the hinges, placed it in the sanctuary, and preached through a sermon series titled "The Open Door Policy." He let the people there know that he would not be in the office much; in fact, it was probably the most ineffective place he could be. His office was going to be their homes and the community at large. He reminded them that John Wesley famously said "the world is my parish."[2]

Without using the specific language, he let them know he would be dividing his time between the center and the edge. This is the 50/50 principle, no matter how many hours we give to the church, we spend 50 percent of our time caring for the existing congregation and 50 percent serving the larger community outside the church.

He visited each member, listening to each member's story and how he or she met Jesus. Some he visited multiple times. The other half of his time, he was out listening in the community, making connections, and encountering the "people of peace" (Luke 10:6). Not everyone was happy with the proposed job description. It defied their image of a conventional minister who was always to be available in the office. It renegotiated the social contract. While some people did leave, others loved being visited in their homes and being heard.

This requires the awareness to see ourselves within our systems. It's to think systemically and personally simultaneously. Adaptive ecclesiology is people focused. It starts with the needs and dreams of the people and builds structures around those needs.

Design Thinking

Design Thinking provides a strong framework for an adaptive approach within inherited systems. This people centered thought model has

2. Richard P. Heitzenrater, *Wesley and the People Called Methodists* (Nashville, TN: Abingdon, 1995), 93.

been widely embraced globally and is being employed across numerous disciplines. Because it is such a flexible methodology, it can be used in any field of work. Some of the most valuable elements for adaptive practice will be frequent iterating based on continuous feedback, through rapid low-resolution prototyping. Ideas are continuously tested in real learning laboratories with real people in the community. We "experiment" with prototypical forms of gatherings within the various third-places.[3]

Design Thinking: This is a model of thought and reflection centered on people. It refers to design-specific cognitive activities that designers apply during the process of designing. This methodology is a new way of thinking and approaching problems, which has become a main issue in contemporary design and discourse. It is widely used as a tool across disciplines.[4]

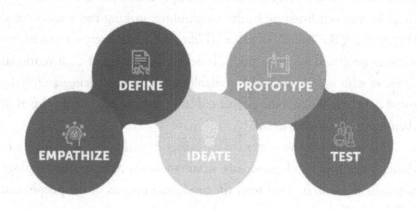

3. Luz Grácio, et al., "Design Thinking in the Scope of Strategic and Collaborative Design," *Strategic Design Research Journal* 10, no. 1 (January 2017): 30–35, 30.

4. Grácio, et al., "Design Thinking in the Scope of Strategic and Collaborative Design," 31.

One prominent motto in this framework, is to "fail early in order to succeed sooner." Failing forward faster is a foundational design thinking principle that helps to maximize learning and insights, crucial for human centered innovation. The focus on collaborative work in small groups, where each individual is fueling the team's creative capacity, is part of the magic of the design thinking process. This scenario map leads to the discussion of solutions, and to the innovation that emerges from the different perspectives given by each person.[5]

Thus, by using the design thinking methodology, it is possible to discover more easily and expediently, through communal experimentation, a potential innovative solution. This tool helps to eradicate the complexity and disorder in the initial stages, which usually paralyze churches from engaging their community. The process allows the team to focus on the essence of the needs of the people; this is innate to the listening, loving, and serving stages of planting a fresh expression.

So, just as the advantage of the design thinking methodology allows designers to immerse themselves in a problem to innovate a potential solution, when applied for our purposes, it enables the team to immerse themselves in the perspective of the people we are seeking to be with. It is in essence an incarnational approach. The emerging forms of church take shape in a collaborative process, where responsibilities are shared among the team and the host culture.

We will simply outline the Design Thinking methodology here, for your team to consider.

Design Thinking Process

Empathize: The team must first gain an empathic understanding of the people we are trying to reach. What struggles do they face, and how can we be withness within those realities? This is not only about consulting experts to analyze a people and their problems, but physically immersing ourselves in their world, so that through relationship we can gain a

---

5.   Grácio, et al., "Design Thinking in the Scope of Strategic and Collaborative Design," 30.

deeper personal understanding of the issues involved. In the fresh expressions journey, this is about listening, then loving and serving.

Define: In the pure design thinking process, this is about the team collecting all the information and processing a problem together. We want to caution here about seeing people in our communities or their life struggles as a problem that the team can solve. Rather, this is more a journey of understanding what's hurting in the community. What are the needs here? What are the opportunities? How do we come together in a mutual exchange of blessing to find healing together? How do we offer communal life with Jesus, and love and serve each other around the sore spots? Who is our other and how can we be with him or her?

Ideate: This is where things get fun! In the pure design thinking process, the team starts generating ideas from the understanding and synthesizing of the users and their needs. For our teams' purposes, this is about asking "What if?" with our eyes toward God's promised hope for the future. There are many techniques to cultivate a healthy brainstorm session, but the main idea is for the team to come up with as many ideas as possible, and nothing is too outside the box. We listened, loved, and served, and began to form relationship with a micro-community. Prayerfully, we now ask how God is calling us to form community with new people, in new places, and in new ways. We suggest drawing people maps, identifying "people of peace," using a fresh expressions process chart, and finding ways to harness technology to generate interest.

Prototype: Again, in the pure process, this stage is about producing inexpensive, smaller versions of a product or its specific features. Many times, prototypes may be shared and tested on a small group of people outside the design team. For our team, this is an experimental phase, in which we get out in the first-, second-, and third-places and simply try stuff. We use prayer walking, and establish a small go team to become an incarnational presence in a space. We pray, observe, and encounter. We form relationships with the "people of peace" who grant access to those spaces. What are the practices of these people and how can they become church? What are the flows that connect them? We then begin experimental gatherings, using those flows to generate awareness.

Test: It's important to remember here that this is a non-linear process, so we remain reflexive as we move through the interweaving stages. It is a fluid process, in which the team will flow and recycle in different directions. The test stage involves iterating frequently based on continuous feedback, experimenting, failing, and using improvisation as you go. Start trying stuff! Can we experiment with a sermonic conversation here? Is music appropriate there? Can we sacramentalize the practice? Are there creative ways to engage people in the space? Is Holy Communion a possibility? We try stuff, see if it works, and adjust. This is an effectual process, rather than a causal one.

Amplification is achieved through *feedback loops*, which begin to transform the whole system. As the team engages in this necessary work of missional experimentation, it pulls the system toward the edge of chaos.

Feedback Loops: These refer to outputs of a system being routed back as inputs, thus forming a loop. Seemingly small inputs eventually magnify into large-scale transformation.[6]

Centered *and* Polycentric Blockchain

The initial mess created in the blended ecology way will ultimately subside, and a new adaptive structural reality will emerge. This new organism will very much be a phenomenon of *emergence*—as synergies interact among the smaller parts and reconfigure in a new whole that is irreducible to the characteristics of those parts.[7] The new composite structural reality will be both centered (hub and spoke) and polycentric (resembling the blockchain).

---

6.   Michael Moynagh, *Church in Life: Emergence, Ecclesiology and Entrepreneurship* (London: SCM, 2017), 22–23.

7.   Vladislav Valentinov, et al., "Emergence: A Systems Theory's Challenge to Ethics," *Systemic Practice & Action Research* 29, no. 6 (2016): 597–610, 597; and Omer Yezdani, et al., "Theory of Emergence: Introducing a Model-Centered Approach to Applied Social Science Research," *Prometheus* 33, no. 3 (2015): 305–322, 306.

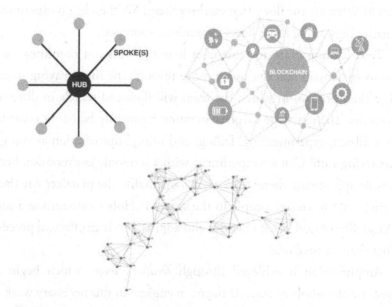

Adaptation occurs through a series of chain reactions of complex synergistic interrelationships. The power source is the very risenness of Jesus. This new remixed organism, a blending of old and new is fundamentally illustrated by the phenomenon of emergence—a force of resurrection. The most compelling image to help us think about how local congregations can envision this emergent structure comes from Jesus's teaching about the vine (John 15).

If you look at the structure of a vineyard, you see a series of rootstocks, or, for our purposes, the inherited church with its centered leadership model, a stable, immobile entity, deeply rooted in the soil. There are also the numerous scions, or wild emerging forms of church, the fresh expressions, with *polycentric*, blockchain structures, which are grafted in, and dependent on, the inherited church rootstock. The vines grow everywhere, forming a complex network. They weave together in such a way that you can no longer distinguish between where one ends and another begins.

In Jesus's parable, he, himself, is the living organism, the true vine, and his synergistic living essence flows through the whole complex network. The Father is the "vinegrower." God is doing the work of pruning, fertilizing, and removing the parts that do not bear fruit. Once again, the focus of Jesus's agrarian metaphors is the expectation of fruit bearing. In this analogy, God is doing all the work! We are the branches; our only function is to abide in a perichoretic union with Jesus. Abiding in Christ, our being with him, results in bearing fruit for him. We are all part of the same vineyard, all connected by Christ himself.

Most inherited congregations function in the hub-and-spoke, centered model of leadership only. This model resembles the rootstock. It's stable, centered, and indispensable. However, what happens when a church begins to experiment with fresh expressions? New scions are grafted in, connected to the rootstock. Yet, they begin to take on a life of their own; mRNA is exchanged, and they are connected in this complex web of life.

Now this analogy allows us to see the ridiculousness of either the attractional or emerging model in isolation. The rootstock cannot really bear fruit until the scion is grafted in. The scion cannot survive and produce fruit without the rootstock. The two need each other. They can produce an incredible harvest when they are blended together. When congregations care for the inherited rootstock and graft in the new scions of fresh expressions, an incredible flourishing harvest is released. All kinds of grapes, of all shapes, sizes, and colors, are blooming everywhere. It is one vine, with many branches and flavors. This is diverse singularity that reflects Trinity.

Synthesizing everything here, to reorganize congregations in this way, we must understand our communities as a larger ecosystem in the way of a vineyard. Jesus is flowing all over the community, there are just places we need to do some grafting, fertilizing, and pruning. The local congregation is like a mini-district with the appointed leader as mini-bishop and missional strategist to the community. Each emerging fresh expression, while connected to the vine, becomes its own kind of church plant.

The inherited congregation as the hub of the activity, the rootstock, needs appropriate care and leadership. The fresh expressions are micro-church plants, connected to, but distinct from, growing wild from the rootstock. The inherited form needs centralized leadership that is appropriate to the leadership framework of the larger system. The fresh expressions are developed within the decentralized, or blockchain, form of shared leadership, expanding to places the rootstock cannot reach, intertwining with the other branches. The priesthood of believers is released to experiment, self-organize, and replicate. Again, the guiding principle here is low initial training, but high ongoing support. This is not about management, controlling, or owning, but about seeding, watering, grafting, and cultivating.

The vineyard shows us how local churches can harness the potential of both hierarchical and networked modes of leadership. The church is gathered and scattered. While the inherited form appreciates and maintains the hierarchal arrangement, the emerging form operates in a decentralized, blockchain arrangement.

J. R. Woodward argues that to create a missional culture in existing congregations we will need "polycentric leadership." He says, "If the church as an institution is going to be missional, I believe the church needs a *polycentric approach to leadership*, where the equippers enable their *fellow priests* to live to their sacred potential. Thus, the entire body is activated for God's mission in the world"[8]

Polycentric Leadership: "Successful communities, even those with long traditions of organized community leadership, will continue to broaden the circles of leadership to create a system for the community that is neither centralized nor decentralized, but rather polycentric. The polycentric view of community leadership assumes that there are many centers of leadership that interrelate."[9]

Again, in our post-industrial Western culture, where pyramids are being replaced by networks, the blended ecology way offers a structure in which the hierarchical and shared leadership modes can operate together. The local church is both congregational and connectional in polity. Leaders are not operating from only one center, but from multiple centers. The

---

8. J. R. Woodward, *Creating a Missional Culture: Equipping the Church for the Sake of the World* (Downers Grove, IL: IVP, 2012), 41.

9. Suzanne Morse, quoted in Woodward, *Creating a Missional Culture*, 60.

latent giftings of the congregation are awakened and released. The blended ecology way as a structural remix futurefits the congregation for resurrection and produces fruit throughout the community.

This enables us to see ourselves within our system. We are living in union with Christ, abiding in him. We are a living expression of the same vineyard, connected by the true vine. When one part of the vineyard flourishes, the whole vineyard benefits. When one part of the vineyard is harmed, the whole vineyard is harmed. We are connected in a symbiotic, organic, and fragile way. The vineyard we call the church is an emergence of which Christ himself is the living, guiding, sustaining force. By the Spirit, we are brought into the life of the Trinity through perichoresis.

Exercise

Fresh Expressions—Design Thinking Micro-cycle

(Re)Defining the Problem: This is about embracing a posture of listening and withness. How do we find creative ways to be the church with people where they are, rather than putting butts in pews?

Need-Finding and Benchmarking: What is "sore" in our community? What are the needs? How can we love and serve? Who is our other and how can we be with him or her?

Ideation: Draw the people map, identify people of peace, and use the fresh expressions process chart in Download 5. How can we harness technology to generate interest?

Prototyping: Pray, observe, and encounter. Get out into the third-places and try stuff. Form relationships with the people of peace who grant access to those spaces. What are the practices of these people and how can they become church? What are the flows that connect them?

Testing: This process involves continuous feedback based on an iterative experience of experimentation, , failure, and improvisation. Start trying stuff! Can we experiment with a sermon here? Is music appropriate? Can we sacramentalize the practice? Are there creative ways to engage people in the space? Is Holy Communion a possibility?

CHAPTER THIRTEEN

"Exceed Thou Authority"

Now during those days, when the disciples were increasing in number, the Hellenists complained against the Hebrews because their widows were being neglected in the daily distribution of food. And the twelve called together the whole community of the disciples and said, 'It is not right that we should neglect the word of God in order to wait on tables. Therefore, brothers and sisters, select from among yourselves seven men of good standing, full of the Spirit and of wisdom, whom we may appoint to this task, while we, for our part, will devote ourselves to prayer and to serving the word.'
—*Acts 6:1-4*

Heifetz, Linsky, and Grashow insist that, in an adaptive challenge, we need to "exceed our authority."

Interestingly, when Bishop Carter ordained me (Michael), he spoke the words: "Take thou authority." This is the charge to those of us ordained to a ministry of the word of God, sacrament, order, and service. We are empowered and authorized to take responsibility to nurture communities of love and forgiveness that do good, and do no harm.

Bishop Carter described the complexity of the adaptive challenge before us and told our class of ordinands: "exceed thou authority."

Blending the Rules

As we travel nationally, working with leaders from many denominations and non-denominatal communities, there comes a time in those gatherings when we get to the institutional questions: How do we measure?

How do we maintain accountability? What about the rules regarding what laity can and can't do? What about sacraments? And the list continues. They are good questions and it's hard to make generalizations that apply to various contexts. But many of them are technical questions, not adaptive ones.

We are in a time when the fate of denominations themselves is in question. When times of shifting paradigms are upon us, like the one we find ourselves in right now, God uses certain people to take risks, bend, blend, and break rules, and to establish new missional norms. You can see this in Jesus's rule-breaking activities within the inherited religious system of his day (Mark 2:23-28 is a pretty clear example). Also, in the book of Acts, the first disciples reframe "the rules" to further the mission (Acts 15). These scenarios reveal that there are times when rules engender conflict with greater missional need and purpose.

Our own Methodist tradition provides a more recent example of this. The reality of a bishop was born from a missional imperative. John Wesley was a person of the "and," someone who remained an Anglican priest until the day he died *and* innovated an entire movement of awakening tethered to the inherited church. He also did a bit of rule blending in his day. As Methodism spread over to the United States and began to take on a life of its own, out of sheer missional necessity, Wesley consecrated Thomas Coke as a "General Superintendent," and then instructed Coke to consecrate Francis Asbury in 1784. Many interpret this action as the defining act that unfortunately created a separate denomination.[1]

Charles Wesley, apparently not too thrilled with this activity, chided his brother in a published poem which read:

So easily are bishops made
    By man's or woman's whim?
W[esley] his hands on C[oke] hath laid,
    But who laid hands on him?[2]

---

1. Richard P. Heitzenrater, *Wesley and the People Called Methodists* (Nashville, TN: Abingdon, 1995), 286–88.

2. Heitzenrater, *Wesley and the People Called Methodists*, 286–88.

These consecrations occurred outside the realm of appropriate authority in the Anglican Church. John Wesley used the scriptural rationale in cases of necessity to validate his actions, and he went back to first principles beneath the traditions. The missional need was primarily to do with providing the sacraments to the new missional frontier. Thus, some blending was in order between the inherited and emerging modes.[3]

Asbury was never comfortable with the title of bishop, and the office today is very different than the role he played. Asbury was an adventurer missionary, who oversaw the work of planting and organizing Methodist circuits to meet the emerging need of the mission field. Many view bishops today as a kind of corporate CEO in the twentieth-century business narrative. However, let's take the concept back to the missional imperative of Wesley's day. A resident bishop is appointed to a specific episcopal "area" as a kind of missional strategist. Missional leaders serve to catalyze movements and organize local leadership to advance the mission.[4]

The most explosive power of the early Methodist movement was the releasing of laity to transform the world. Wesley took "ordinary heroes" among the priesthood of all believers and called them "lay preachers."[5] The different Methodist gatherings were sustained by the laity. At first, these leaders were chosen by Wesley and commissioned to serve in different capacities.[6] This allowed for a recovery of the APEST, as apostles, prophets, evangelists, shepherds, and teachers were released to serve as the people of God. They were unleashed into the fields, prisons, and mining communities, as well as into the societies, classes, bands, and Methodist preaching houses.

Wesley was an apostolic leader who advanced the gospel and pioneered entire systems, while sustaining the larger institution's integrity. He was a gifted mess-maker and master of improvisational leadership.

---

3. Heitzenrater, *Wesley and the People Called Methodists*, 286–88.

4. Alan Hirsch and Tim Catchim, *The Permanent Revolution: Apostolic Imagination and Practice for the 21st Century Church* (San Francisco: Jossey-Bass, 2012), 214.

5. Heitzenrater, *Wesley and the People Called Methodists*, 113.

6. Heitzenrater, *Wesley and the People Called Methodists*, 118–19.

Innovating missional movements among inherited systems often creates a polarity between competing truths. The people called Methodists were born from a missional impulse that ultimately led to the creation of a whole new institution. Adventurers usually feel faced with a choice: either to leave the inherited system and start from scratch, or to work within the inherited system that we know and love to bring revival. If we choose the latter, at some point, we will find ourselves in the position Wesley did. John Wesley chose mission over strict adherence to rules that confined the Gospel's expansion, and yet he maintained integrity within the institution. He did some rule blending.

Again, as Bolsinger reminds us: "when you go off the map, the rules change."[7] As we engage the communities where we live and plant fresh expressions throughout the ecosystem, situations will arise that call for adventurers to make decisions. Some of the rules will seem confining and, at the end of the day, we will ultimately have to be responsive to the Spirit.

However, we have been innovating within an inherited system throughout our ministries, and we have always discovered creative ways to advance the mission while maintaining faithfulness to the covenant we made at our ordinations. Of course, we've done some rule *blending* between the inherited and emerging modes along the way. Let's lean into the wisdom of Gil Rendle here.

Rendle asks, "Can David and Goliath live together?" or more specifically, "Can a movement live inside an institution?" He reminds us that institutions and movements are not at war with each other and, as we have gone to great lengths to demonstrate, one is not right and the other wrong. We must remember to be conjunctive people, here—people of the "and." Institutions and movements are a polarity: two competing truths held together in tension. Both are good and necessary.[8]

7.   Tod Bolsinger, *Canoeing the Mountains: Christian Leadership in Uncharted Territory* (Downers Grove, IL: IVP, 2018), 191.

8.   Gil Rendle, *Back to Zero: The Search to Rediscover the Methodist Movement* (Nashville, TN: Abingdon, 2011), 83.

Rendle argues that the appropriate response to polarity is not to pick a side, but to manage the tension in the middle. This is exactly what the blended ecology is all about, and why there is an intentional focus on grafting the two organisms together. The inherited and emerging modes of church are one in the same vine in one in the same vineyard. We don't need to choose one, we need to embrace both and live in the creative tension. It also reveals why it is so hard for people in the two forms to understand each other. A polarity map reveals that the longer one is aligned with one of the extremes, the less value they will see in the competing truth.[9]

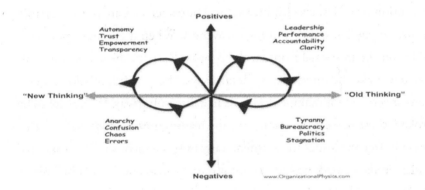

Rendle offers a criterion for rule breaking to help us live in the tension. He takes this concept from a retired army general who realized that, on that battlefield, as nascent situations arise, new developing strategies may become appropriate that require a leader to break the rules. Even in an extreme institution like the military, with strict protocols, procedures, and clear chains of command, good leaders may need to adopt a posture of improvisation and break rank to win the battle.[10]

---

9.   Rendle, *Back to Zero*, 84.

10.   Rendle, *Back to Zero*, 29.

This doesn't mean the leaders should run willy-nilly, breaking rules at will. In fact, there should be as much discipline in breaking rules as there is in following them. The leader should carefully consider criteria that thoughtfully address purpose before breaking any rule.

These are the three questions to ask when considering breaking a rule:

1. What is the purpose of the rule?
2. Is the rule still appropriate?
3. Does the rule serve or prevent the mission?[11]

While we can appreciate the rootedness, depth, and structure that an institution provides, clunky, hierarchical bureaucracies are not necessarily known for agility, speed, and responsiveness. When it comes to new situations on the missional frontier, the people closest to the action must ultimately make the decisions. As Rendle says, "Purposeful, missional questions are critical for making decisions in a discerning way. If rules are to be broken, there must be a reason, and the reason must be missional."[12] This does not free the leader to act unilaterally or spontaneously. The missional leader needs to work within the local frameworks, and "publicize" his or her intent to change or veer from the rule before acting.[13]

For followers of Jesus, we can add another threefold matrix to guide our missional decision-making. Steven Croft notes a three-way conversation that needs to take place that can guide the missional practice of mixed economy church life:

1. The new community (the emerging needs of the fresh expression).
2. The primary values articulated in scripture (the "first principles" breathing forth from the word).

---

11. Rendle, *Back to Zero*, 20.

12. Rendle, *Back to Zero*, 29.

13. Rendle, *Back to Zero*, 30.

3. The received tradition or denomination from which the new community is emerging (values of the inherited congregation).[14]

While we need to honor the inherited system, operate within it, and always act with integrity, in a sense, if we really love the inherited church, we will need to do some rule blending. At the very least, we've got some boundary pushing to do. Maybe leaders are people who just love God and neighbor enough that they are willing to blend the rules. The guiding word of this activity always come back to the mission; as Bishop Ken Carter preached to group of ordinands coming into ministry amidst polarization, division and exhaustion, "Nothing is sacred but the Mission".

Or as Tod Bolsinger says, "the mission trumps!"[15]

The mission trumped for Jesus, the early church, Mary the Apostle of Apostles, and John Wesley. May the mission trump for us, as well. The blended ecology allows us to serve the institutional church faithfully, while responding to the missional opportunities that arise before us.

Futurefitting Leadership Roles— Mini-Bishops

Obviously, for this to work at the grassroots level, we need to reorganize the local church around the single imperative of mission. Alan Hirsch says that "every believer ought to be considered a church planter and every church should be thought of as a church-planting church."[16] If we survey the structural reality of the early church in the New Testament, we see a diffusion of authority among the disciples. Hirsch reminds us of the movemental nature of the early church, which was sustained through shared leadership, not centralized power (more blockchain, than hub-and-spoke). We need to recover those movement dynamics, which "require

---

14. Steven Croft, *Mission-Shaped Questions: Defining Issues for Today's Church* (New York: Seabury, 2010), 196.

15. Bolsinger, *Canoeing the Mountains*, 123.

16. Hirsch and Catchim, *The Permanent Revolution*, 209.

that power and function flow away from the center to the outermost limits, giving the whole movement a profoundly centrifugal feel."[17]

The APEST is not about "leadership." We are "ordained" into our roles in the APEST in the waters of our baptism. Every Christian serves a function within the body. Every Christian is a leader, and some specific leadership roles are a calling from among this common calling. On the new missional frontier, we must discern practical ways to equip every believer to cultivate his or her APEST gifting.

Chris Backert, Director of Fresh Expressions US, says that for the blended ecology to work, local pastors will have to accept their role as mini-bishops. In the biblical sense, the various leadership roles(elders, deacons, bishops, etc.) emerged improvisationally in the process of mission. The "ordination" of these leaders was quite different than how ordination works in an institutional sense. The first disciples were set apart to serve, but in response to an emerging missional imperative. Denominations have taken the three scriptural concepts of leadership and arranged them in a pyramidal corporate hierarchy.

Steven Croft discusses the danger of embracing the corporate concept of "leadership" wholesale. Croft advocates for a rediscovery of the value of these three leadership roles. He associates the three groups in the following ways: (1) deacon (diakonia), the servant ministry of the church with pioneers; (2) elder (presbyteros), the priestly function of the church enabling and sustaining both inherited and emerging forms of church; and (3) bishop (episcope), the one who watches over the church; bishops are those who exercise collaborative oversight of areas with multiple parishes. Croft also argues that we continue to need lay, licensed, and ordained individuals for the full health of the mixed economy.[18]

The scriptural origins of these three roles have taken on new dimensions in the denominational scenario. In the blended ecology, this larger denominational structure needs to be re-appropriated and remixed for the

---

17. Hirsch and Catchim, *The Permanent Revolution*, 210.

18. Steven J. Croft, *The Future of the Parish System: Shaping the Church of England for the Twenty-first Century* (London: Church House, 2006), 78–90.

local church. Thus, the roles of adventurer, advocate, and authorizer are closer to the "first principles" of the leadership roles that emerged improvisationally in the process of mission. This is a fitting way to understand how local church pastors will need to restructure the leadership of existing congregations. Do we need bishops on the emerging mission field? Absolutely. In fact, in this sense, all inherited clergy persons should understand themselves in this role . . . as mini-bishops to our larger community.

No longer can we clergy confine our roles to the local congregation. We must expand our responsibilities to the surrounding areas as a chief missional strategist. The role of local clergy people must expand to include equipping, commissioning, and releasing local leaders to their contexts. They must be serving the priesthood of believers as they plant churches throughout the neighborhoods and networks. This requires local clergy to be more like catalyzers and equippers than personal butlers to an existing group or institutional machinists.

Covenant

A covenant can be an effective way to establish boundaries around this emerging missionary force. This should reflect the unique local context, but the team members should hammer this out together and everyone sign on to it. Creating a covenant with your leaders helps you get clear about your guiding values, discern together appropriate boundaries, and give a leader recourse when something goes haywire. The covenant should include a commitment to personal holiness and establish how team members will relate to one another. The repercussions for violating this covenant should be established up front as well.

On the Job Training

One of the things that was spoken into me, and now I speak regularly into our emerging leaders, is this: "God does not call the qualified, God qualifies the called." Jesus did not send his disciples to seminary. He did not put them through psychological evaluations, undertake gift inventories, or provide character reference forms. Jesus would not be considered a good leader by most standards today. I think Jesus relied heavily on trusting the Holy Spirit. He shaped his disciples in the process of becoming. While it is true that God doesn't always call the qualified, the local church has a responsibility to form people to do good, and more specifically to do no harm. This is its own kind of relational and organic qualification process.

Essentially, the most important undergirding principle to this whole endeavor is to trust the Holy Spirit who provides every gift and bestows all powers.

When it comes to fresh expressions lay ministers, people often note how exceptionally gifted they are. Many fresh expressions ministers have no undergraduate degrees and most have no formal seminary education. They often have no previous experience in ministry, and they have usually completed no credentialing process. Yet, they preach, teach, pastor, evangelize, and apostle at a level that is at least consistent with seminary-educated, ordained clergy people. Why is this?

The Holy Spirit is the short answer. This is because ordination processes do not make disciples of Jesus. Neither do seminaries. Neither do licensing schools. Neither do education, referrals, or psychological evaluations. While those processes are valuable and make us better, the Holy Spirit makes disciples. Period. They are functioning at the level they are because of a combination of two things: (1) following the Holy Spirit, and (2) having opportunities to use their gifts. That's it.

That's what the disciples had. It's called on-the-job training. Jesus's disciples had no seminary, no formal training plan, not even a twelve-week membership class. It's fascinating to move through the Gospels and to see Jesus's shaky leadership development plan. It was a little bit of "Come follow me," and then a whole lot of "We'll figure this out as we go." The disciples have great moments of success, embarrassing blunders, and epic failures—all in the process of following Jesus. They become disciples by being disciples. They become sent ones in the process of sentness.

As J. R. Woodward says, "one of the ways we can teach reliance on the Holy Spirit to our fellow priests is by moving from dependence on a solo pastor or senior pastor to dependence on the Spirit through polycentric leadership."[19]

Releasing is all about relying on the Holy Spirit.

Clergy Who Practice Retiring

Roland Allen, speaking of Paul's missionary methods, wrote, "He gave as a right to the Spirit-bearing body the powers which duly belong to the Spirit-bearing body. He gave freely, and then he retired from them that they might learn to exercise the powers which they possessed in Christ"[20]

Jesus practiced retiring. When his disciples were so busy they forgot to eat, he said things like, "Come away with me to a quiet place, let's rest" and "You give them something to eat" (Mark 6:31, 37). Paul regularly practiced retiring. He would go and plant movements, organize local leadership, and then move onto to the next town. Sure, he still had to jump in and try to correct the communities he planted frequently, but he intentionally practiced releasing local leadership, and then moving on.

Research conducted in the United Kingdom on pioneer ministry demonstrates that "adventurers leave." This does not always mean they jump from church to church; it means they initiate, start, and launch ventures, and then move to the next venture. This can be done from the same local parish for years. Mature innovators learn to establish relational networks that sustain their innovations. They work alongside advocates and authorizers, co-creating together. This allows indigenous

---

19. J. R. Woodward, *Creating a Missional Culture: Equipping the Church for the Sake of the World* (Downers Grove, IL: IVP, 2012), 213.

20. Roland Allen, *Missionary Methods: St. Paul's or Ours* (Grand Rapids, MI: Eerdmans, 1962), 149.

leaders to emerge, and for the whole apostlehood to have an active leadership role.

Adventurers cultivate a process of ecclesial innovation. This involves the journey of dissatisfaction, exploration, sense-making, amplification, and reaching the edge of chaos, which leads to transformation. The community itself lives out and sustains this transformation; they adopt the new way. Why? Because nothing is sacred but the mission.

CHAPTER FOURTEEN

Go

In *Structured for Mission*, Alan J. Roxburgh explains that Eurotribal denominations are experiencing a major identity crisis. The corporate, legitimating narrative that once helped them thrive is no longer valid.[1] Local churches are not properly structured for a post-Christendom scenario. Roxburgh challenges the false notion of pitting the Spirit against structure, as if those two are in opposition. The Spirit both flows through inherited structures and disrupts them when necessary. God is the primary agent of disruption when we have adopted false legitimating narratives and created systems that operate based in faulty assumptions.[2]

Roxburgh demonstrates that God being the primary active agent in disruption is a recurring theme throughout scripture. From the exodus to the exile, to the sending of the church, and, ultimately, to the core of all disruption, we see an adaptive ecclesiology. When displacements occur, they create dissatisfaction and an opportunity for the church to harness the Spirit's disruptive power in the liminal space, to build in time to improvise, innovate, and cultivate new habits and practices.[3]

When God disrupts our sin-broken cycles of decline and decay, the people are released to fresh imaginations and visions, and new structures are birthed. Roxburgh describes the "hub and spoke" institutional structure,

---

1. Alan J. Roxburgh, *Structured for Mission: Renewing the Culture of the Church* (Downers Grove, IL: InterVarsity, 2015), 77–79.

2. Roxburgh, *Structured for Mission*, 25.

3. Roxburgh, *Structured for Mission*, 51.

which denominations adopted from twentieth-century corporate America. This corporate model assumes a "central hub," where power is centralized and then flows from the center down the spokes of the wheel.[4] The hub-and-spoke structure alone is ineffective. We need a remix.

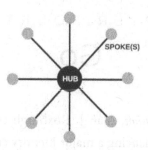

For instance, many denominations and general agencies have headquarters based in a strategically located city, from whence the professionals dispense leadership, resources, and expertise to the local churches. The power is centralized in the hub, where strategies are decided and then implemented throughout the system. The corporate narrative undergirding this structure is based in hierarchy, efficiency, and centralized control. Causal rationality reigns supreme.

In this system, rewards are doled out to those who play the corporate game well and oil the institutional machine. Roxburgh argues that this structure can never effectively ascertain and respond to the challenges being faced by local contexts.[5]

Roxburgh does not call for dismantling denominations and the inherited systems, rather he sees them as instrumental to the future of the church. He advocates for the restructuring of the "hub and spoke," by breaking free of the corporate narrative of centralized power and expertise, and releasing local contexts to grassroots, dispersed, and networked

---

4.   Roxburgh, *Structured for Mission*, 119.

5.   Roxburgh, *Structured for Mission*, 119.

innovation and experimentation.[6] This is the bottom-up, self-organizing kind of emergence that our innovative frameworks lead to.

Futurefitting Starts with a Team

As the inherited form of church continues to function primarily in the hub-and-spoke model, futurefitting begins with the formation of a team. This Pasteur-like, onsite laboratory breaks the toxic loop and infects the congregation with the missional virus.

It doesn't have to be a big team. *Amplification* is about making small changes that release a trophic cascade of transformation. In our experience, mission is like a virus that spreads throughout the body, but it must start somewhere. Creating a small team specifically for that function is essential. This is the disruptive innovation department of your church.

In Jesus's missional blueprint, Luke 10:1-9, we see Jesus's approach as an effectual strategy, not a causal one. Teams of two are sent out to find "people of peace," starting with who and what they have, traveling lightly, responding to emergent realities as they unfold, leveraging contingencies, and so on. The key here is to start with who and what you already have. Jesus transformed the world by sending out disciples in teams of two. You, another person, and the Holy Spirit make a team.

On the new missional frontier, there is no room for heroic solo leaders. From an effectuation perspective, we know successful entrepreneurs are concerned less about having the "right people," and more about nurturing the people you already have in your sphere of influence. This is also Jesus's way.

At Wildwood, Michael simply turned a dwindling Evangelism Committee into the Fresh Expressions Team, and he trained them minimally. Then, this newly-formed team generated excitement and interest from those who were experiencing dissatisfaction. Some people showed up just out of curiosity to see what Fresh Expressions was about. With this new

---

6. Roxburgh, *Structured for Mission*, 136.

energy, using the design thinking approach, and under the guidance of the Holy Spirit, the team began experimentally to launch multiple fresh expressions in the surrounding community.

Over time, Wildwood became reformed in the blended ecology way though the small experimental changes of this team. The facility became a missional outpost with little micro-community movements all around. Think of a starfish with a body of five arms radially arranged around a central disk reaching out, influencing the community in multiple directions at once. Every time you cut a piece off the starfish, the severed piece regenerates a new starfish.

This apostolic team soon began to discover other adventurers out on the missional edge. They were innovators, trying to embody God's love with non-Christians, but without the language, training, and support of the Fresh Expressions movement. They quickly began to connect with these people, pool resources, and work together. We refer to this as "strategic partnerships."

Jesus took people who knew how to fish and said, "I will show you how to fish for people." He took people's natural skillset and their circle of influence and trained them how to use those natural inclinations, intrinsic motivations, and abilities to expand God's kingdom. He also patiently labored beside them, as they failed-forward and became the people he created them to be.

Likely, any church has the capacity to organize a fresh expressions team. This team of people should have a gifting in these three primary roles: adventurer, advocate, and authorizer.

As the team grows, you will need all three of these kinds of folks on the team. Scripturally, we can see these roles in the life of the Apostle Paul. Paul was obviously an adventurer, comfortable on the edges, planting the seeds of the Gospel there. But Paul also had a Barnabas or two, the encouragers who were advocates of the work and traveling with Paul. Paul also had an Ananias, who healed Paul of his blindness and authorized him to become the apostle to the Gentiles in his commissioning. Furthermore, sometimes supporters and permission-givers are retired adventurers! As Paul matured in his apostolic role, he became an authorizer and advocate himself to his many Timothys.

Core, Fringe of the Core, Fringe

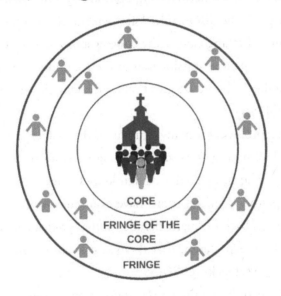

As the team develops, it's helpful to think in terms of three relational dimensions. You want your solid and devoted Christians, those who are mature in their faith,—the "core" of the team, if you will. But you also want to have some people on this team who are newer Christians, and maybe not even members of your church. Maybe they are just exploring. Inviting these people on the "fringe of the core" is vital. They often still have connections with relational networks in the community and may even have access to the people of peace. Finally, you do want to have people on the team who may or may not even be Christian. These are people on the "fringe." These folks most likely have no connection to your church at all. They may even become the people of peace themselves. They may be the ones who open access to the third-places in the community.

50/50: Tending the Tree—AND— Experimenting in the Garden

Borrowing again from the wisdom of Alan Roxburgh, we must carve out time for local experimentation. This activity can start small. As amplification takes root, the inherited congregation is reconfigured. A good and simple principle is the 50/50 rule. Fifty percent of our time needs to be structured toward taking care of the congregation, and the other 50 percent needs to be spent as missionaries in the community. That means for whatever number of hours we give time to the church, we need to divide our time in this way.

A growing problem for many churches is the inability to support full-time clergy. Full-time pastors are becoming a luxury to most congregations. Anyone who has served a church knows "there's no such thing as a part-time pastor." Congregations have expectations of their ministers, some that stream back for many decades to the "golden age" of Christendom. There is an expectation that the pastor is always on call. This is a harmful culture that lacks resilience.

Clergy need to be released from those expectations and renegotiate the social contract.

Without good self-care, sabbath, and prioritizing family over work, serving in any ministry is not sustainable. Regarding the 50/50 principle, clergy need to set good boundaries with congregations. Provide a weekly schedule that breaks down your time. Build sabbath and family time into that schedule. In addition, clearly delineate the 50 percent of your time that will be spent cultivating the inherited congregation, and the other 50 percent you will be spending out in the community at large. Build into that time space to simply be in third-places, to pray, observe, and encounter. Consistent presence in those spaces can open all kinds of opportunities. Clergy are not called to serve a congregation only, but a whole community.

This is not just a good principle for the appointed leader. The leader is modeling the behavior we want to see manifest in all staff and the congregation at large. Everyone in the church must divide his or her time in the 50/50 way. The leaders of the congregation are establishing behavioral patterns in the congregation through modeling. One simple way to live into this, even during demanding weeks filled with disruptions, is to do as many internal church functions as possible out in the community. Rather than doing everything at the compound, go to restaurants, parks, coffee shops, and so on. Everything you can do out in the community or in someone's home, do it!

Increasingly, there are more and more bi-vocational clergy—tentmakers like Paul the Apostle. There is now a growing number of co-vocational clergy, those who turn their normal workplace into church. *Bi-vocational*, with the prefix *bi-* as in *twice, double,* or *dual,* literally means "two voices" or callings, and it describes people who serve a local church and maintain employment at another job. *Co-vocational*, with the prefix *co-* as in *with* or *together,* literally means "with voice" or a "with-ness" calling, and it describes people who turn their workplaces into church. Every Christian has the capacity to be a co-vocational minister.

As this transition occurs, local churches will increasingly serve as a kind of seminary for the apostlehood of all believers. What if Sunday School and Bible studies were repurposed as "underground seminaries" in which clergy give away their expensive educations to their people for free? Education processes in the local church must be focused less on sitting and learning and refocused on practical training for mission to the local community.

These are all ways to get outside our comfort zones and live on the edge.

CHAPTER FIFTEEN
People Fear Loss, Not Change

The whole congregation of the Israelites complained against Moses and Aaron
in the wilderness. The Israelites said to them, "If only we had died by the hand
of the Lord in the land of Egypt, when we sat by the pots of meat and ate
our fill of bread, for you have brought us out into this wilderness
to kill this whole assembly with hunger."
—Exodus 16:2-3

In the history of evangelism there was a geographical space in the United States that came to be known as the "burned over district." One evangelist after another had passed through the region. Many had been converted, some on multiple occasions. The excitement was palpable. And, then, many among these communities would fall away, and there became a residual skepticism.

We could blame this outcome as being the result of an inadequate discipleship system, or on having a truncated definition of *sanctification*. We could also learn from history. Churches do not exist in a vacuum. We practice evangelism in a particular context and history. Understanding all of this is a part of the diagnosis. It is what we see when we get up into the balcony. We discover historical, social, and cultural movements.

When the next evangelists and witnesses come along, how do we respond when we are living in our own burned over districts? This is a critical question for the adaptive church. We claim the truth, power, and goodness of Jesus's message. We are consistent in proclaiming the message of all that God has done for us, and we are flexible in the mission of how we share that and with whom. We listen. We diagnose. We stay a bit longer in the balcony before we plunge into the interventions of activity and judgment.

Adaptive Change Is Loss

Adaptive change involves loss. Technical change is the avoidance of loss. Given our human nature, most of us would choose to avoid loss. Loss is typically related to pain, disorientation, and the journey to becoming whole once again.

One of our temptations, as Gil Rendle reminds us, is toward nostalgia. We remember the past with a kind of selective memory. As life proceeds, inevitable change introduces us to loss. We can lament that loss, or we live in denial about it. Or, we can adapt.

The stable and homogeneous family is in the memory of many church leaders. This form of family was at the heart of the post-World War II church. Many of us grew up in these families. Some of us did not. And our remembrance of these families can be inaccurate—often for the purpose of self-protection.

Adaptive change is a reckoning with the loss of this kind of family in the United States. Young adults are taking many more years to begin families. Many of these young adults experienced brokenness in their own families of origin and are more deliberative in beginning their own journeys toward commitment. A nostalgia might blame them. An empathy might seek to understand them. An adaptation would further attempt to include them in the life of God's mission.

The stable and homogenous family has been disestablished in much the same way the traditional mainline church has been. Indeed, these two realities are linked. We might mourn this as a loss while confessing that neither is essential to God's mission in our world. God loves the world,

143

God uses the church as an instrument of mission, and God desires that we are in connection with each other. It is not good that we are alone. The shape of church and family are contextual, and the values of each are shaped and sanctified by an ongoing encounter with Jesus, who calls us to love one another, and with the presence of the Holy Spirit, which bears fruit in our life together.

Would people really "rather die than change"? Katy Milkman studied adaptation and why change seems so difficult. In her research she discovered,

> It turns out that the leading cause of premature death isn't poor health care, difficult social circumstances, bad genes, or environmental toxins. Instead, an estimated 40 percent of premature deaths are the result of personal behaviors we can change. I'm talking about daily, seemingly small decisions about eating, drinking, exercise, smoking, sex, and vehicle safety. These decisions add up, producing hundreds of thousands of fatal cancers, heart attacks, and accidents each year.[1]

Milkman came upon an incredibly important but underappreciated insight: "If you want to change your behavior or someone else's, you're at a huge advantage if you begin with a blank slate—a fresh start—and no old habits working against you."[2] Unfortunately, in most congregations we are dealing with decades of old habits, mental models, and skewed assumptions. We often don't get to have a start fresh.

Milkman learned that you didn't necessarily need a fresh start if there was a way to harness the feeling of a blank slate, even in moments when no true tabula rasa existed. These one-way movements, like Fresh Expressions, are gifts to the church. When congregations start new faith communities together it renews the sense of purpose. It enables an experiment to take place that is a new beginning for those involved. New life starts to spill out into the parish, and also into the existing congregation.

1. Katy Milkman *How to Change: The Science of Getting from Where You Are to Where You Want to Be* (New York: Portfolio, 2021), 15.

2. Milkman, *How to Change*, 19.

It also introduces daily, seemingly small decisions and habits into the life of the church again: listening, loving, building relationships, sharing Jesus, and so on. The small habits, lived out in the new experiment, feed back into the common life of the existing church. Like someone with a fatal heart condition, the new behaviors enable us to cooperate with the healing following a bypass surgery. Like new exercise and eating habits, we practice one day at a time. The positive learnings and new relationships begin slowly to overcome the fear of loss.

The loss is real. And, yet, the loss is for the sake of a gift that God wants to give to us. Some of the loss is a shedding, a detachment from things that are not of God. And the courage inherent in an adaptive ecclesiology puts us in touch with an ancient movement—the apostolic church.